FIVE LECTURES

— ON —

FORMAL
AXIOLOGY

Robert S. Hartman

FIVE LECTURES

ON

FORMAL
AXIOLOGY

ROBERT S. HARTMAN

FOREWORD BY CLIFFORD G. HURST

IZZARD INK
PUBLISHING

IZZARD INK PUBLISHING COMPANY
PO Box 522251
Salt Lake City, Utah 84152
www.izzardink.com

LIBRARY OF CONGRESS CONTROL NUMBER:2019936191

Designed by Izzard Ink Publishing
Cover Design LaceyAnn Kisko Design

First Edition April 23, 2019

Contact the author at info@izzardink.com

Softback ISBN: 978-1-64228-026-5
eBook ISBN: 978-1-64228-027-2

CONTENTS

PREFACE

During the final decade or so of his life, Hartman frequently delivered a series of lectures in which he outlined the need for a value theory, the theoretical requirements demanded of an effective value theory, and his rationale behind the development of his value theory, known as formal axiology.

He named these lectures, collectively, *Five Lectures on Formal Axiology.*

It is not known when these lecture notes were first written or delivered, but it is clear that Hartman revised them regularly. Although the lectures are not dated, the current monograph, I believe, represents his most "final" version of them. Lecture V describes an anecdote from an article that was published in Reader's Digest in April of 1973. This was less than five months before Hartman's death in late September of that same year.

The Institute previously published these five lectures in serial form in Volumes X and XI of the *Journal of Formal Axiology: Theory and Practice.* By bringing them together, in one volume, we are able to offer to readers the clearest, most cogent, and most concise description of his theory, in his own words, that Hartman ever wrote.

If you have ever been put off by the sheer mass and intellectual density of either *The Structure of Value* or *The Knowledge of Good*, then you will find these Five Lectures to be a breath of fresh air. Written as they were for oral delivery, they have a cadence and clarity to them that make them a pleasure to read.

—Clifford G. Hurst

Editor

FOREWORD

by Clifford G. Hurst

Robert S. Hartman [1910-1973] is best known today—to the extent that he is known—for his development
of the Hartman Value Profile (HVP). While the HVP is
increasingly being used by consultants, counselors, and ex-
ecutive coaches around the globe, the theory on which it
is based—Hartman's theory of formal axiology—remains
unfamiliar to many people. It deserves a broader audience.

Hartman's intellectual pursuits extended far beyond
this theory and this instrument. He also wrote about,
and advocated for, employee benefits, profit sharing,
new forms of capitalism, new approaches to international relations, nuclear disarmament, spirituality, and world
peace.

Hartman was a prolific writer, but many of his best
thoughts never saw the light of day during his lifetime.

Shortly after Hartman's unexpected and untimely
death in 1973, his widow, Rita Hartman, wrote to their
friend John Davis:

I can comprehend that the life I helped to build
has reached an end, but what overwhelms me and
hurts more than anything else is to see the abundance of unfinished publications lying fallow. I am
almost obsessed with the idea that somehow this
must be utilized, it must go on, it must be used.

In 1976 the Robert S. Hartman Institute for Formal
and Applied Axiology was founded as a not-for-profit corporation in order to preserve, refine, advance, and make
better known to the world the work begun by Hartman.
See the Institute's website: www.hartmaninstitute.org,
for a complete statement of its mission and purpose.

Hartman's autobiography, *Freedom to Live*, was published
posthumously by the Institute in 1994. A second edition was
published in 2013. Its re-publication marked the first volume in the planned *Hartman Institute Axiology Studies* series.

The current and future monographs in this series
continue the Institute's intention to fulfill Rita Hartman's wishes that this work "must go on."

Archival research which resulted in discovering and
digitally capturing many of the monographs in this series
was made possible, in part, by Gore Summer Research
Grants provided to two students and a faculty member
of Westminster College during the summer of 2018. We
are grateful for this support.

The Institute would also like to thank Arthur R. Ellis
and Charlotte B. Ellis for their generous financial contri-
bution which has made the publication of these monographs possible.

Lecture I

VALUE AS A
SCIENTIFIC OBJECT

ABSTRACT

In this lecture, Hartman argued that beginning with the Renaissance era, natural philosophy was separated from philosophy by creating and applying mathematics to its empirical subject matter, thereby evolving into real natural sciences like physics and chemistry. Unfortunately, there has been no parallel development in moral philosophy or in value theory—axiology—more generally. Because values are not empirical objects, ethics (and other value disciplines) must become formal sciences that address their subject matter through their own logic, and discern and apply their own formal patterns. When completed, this will become the science of Formal Axiology, which Hartman says he will begin to develop in subsequent lectures.

Let us begin our discussion by tracing the problem of value to its historic sources. The subtleties of axiological discussion are not an end in themselves, but a means of understanding moral reality. Our current world situation is a moral situation par excellence; for it is the first universal situation in history where the lack of ethical knowledge itself is felt to be the main—and disastrous—characteristic of the human condition.

It is commonplace today that we suffer from a moral and intellectual disequilibrium: the anguish and uncertainty of our age, we know, is due to the discrepancy between our knowledge of nature, on the one hand, and our ignorance of morality, on the other. Natural philosophy, in the form of natural science, has developed methods which have brought gigantic natural forces within the reach of any individual capable of pulling a switch or pushing a button. It has given man control of the cosmic force itself and enabled him either to blow up the planet or to bring it unheard-of abundance.

The choice between these two alternatives—and the choice must be made—depends on the development of moral philosophy. But moral philosophy has not developed as has its twin, natural philosophy. The natural philosophers of the Renaissance, Kepler, Galileo, Newton, Descartes, Leibniz, and others, who invented the tools of natural science, changed our world from an unconnected multitude of secluded villages and walled-in cities into a connected unit, interlaced by telephones and cables, railroad tracks and highways, air and sea lanes, sound and light waves. Natural philosophy has changed the face of the earth to such an extent that neither Julius Caesar nor Columbus would recognize it. Unfortunately, Jesus Christ would recognize it only too well. For, the inner world in which he was interested and where he hoped to establish the Kingdom of God, looks as barren and sterile, as chaotic and anarchic, as neglected and uncultivated as in his day. While physical nature has yielded to man's inquiring mind and is opening up to him ever richer treasures, man's inner nature is a wasteland he has never bothered to explore with equal determination. Here, in this vast region within a man and between men, much of the work of cultivation is still to be done—the clearing and plowing, the building of highways and lines of communication. Here is a field to till, a harvest to reap, treasures to unlock, resources to mobilize and energies to free, which may well match those of material nature.

As it is, we are living in several ages at once. With our emotions we are still in the Stone Age, hating and loving, envying and desiring as primitively as the caveman, and, from time to time, breaking through the thin veneer of civilization with unheard-of savagery. Yet, with our intellect we are organizing planetary travel. Our political institutions are rooted in the eighteenth century and some of our so-called modern societies use devices of classical tyranny if not tribal cannibalism; and yet, we are building the atomic plants of the next century. We have lost control even of our own inventions and have thus magnified our chaotic emotions to global if not cosmic dimensions. We have made our world a paradox: artificial satellites whirl around us, yet deep within us are frozen in the fear of a cosmic explosion. We have made our world a monstrosity: in the dungeons of some of our "governments" the noiseless efficiency of techniques is mixed with the groaning of tortured men and women. We suffer from moral schizophrenia: man, in the words of Nietzsche, is a rope stretched between beast and superman; one more tug, and the rope will snap—the supermen will revert to beasts. To one society this has happened in our time, and it is likely to happen to any nation if technological societies do not mobilize their moral energies; if they do not match their technical efficiency with moral intelligence.

Philosophers have recognized for some time that the only way to bring order out of the present chaos of the

moral disciplines—and hence the world of human relations—is to make the same kind of systematic analysis
of moral phenomena and moral thinking that was made
by the founders of natural science in the field of natural phenomena and factual thinking. Just as the natural
philosophers developed mathematics as a tool for understanding nature, so moral philosophers have been trying
to develop a tool for understanding moral nature. This
tool is called Axiology or value theory.

The quest into the meaning of value is of relatively recent date. Before Kant the fundamental difference
between natural philosophy and moral philosophy was
hardly recognized, and the equally fundamental difference between philosophy and science is largely unknown even to this day. Both are methods which are still
confused with their contents. It is not recognized that
there may be moral science as there is natural science,
and that moral philosophy is to moral science as natural philosophy is to natural science, e.g. as alchemy is to
chemistry or astrology to astronomy. Even in the natural
disciplines it took a long time until the distinction between natural philosophy and natural science was made.
The natural philosophers as late as the last century did
not yet know—or like—the new name "scientist;" and
Faraday despised it as much as the 'new-fangled' term
'physicist.' "I was formerly a bookseller and binder but
now am a philosopher,"… he remarked. "When an ap-
prentice, I for amusement learned a little chemistry and

other parts of philosophy." Laboratories were then still called "philosophical," and performed "philosophical experiments" with "philosophical instruments." In other words, science had not yet consciously outgrown the leading-strings of philosophy. The tradition of Newton, whose *Mathematical Principles of Natural Philosophy* had laid the foundation of the whole development, was still completely alive, even though Laplace had eliminated one of the fundamental "hypotheses" of the Newtonian system, God, since *je n'avais pas boson in de cette hypothèse-la,* "I didn't need that hypothesis." Only by the end of the 19th century and the first half of the 20th century did science, as such, come into its own; and the fundamental difference between its method and that of philosophy has not been thoroughly, or logically, investigated even yet.

Moral philosophy, of course, was even more "philosophical" than natural philosophy, and has remained so to this day, even though large segments of what a hundred years ago was called moral philosophy have since developed into the so-called social sciences and the humanities. Only metaphysics, ethics, aesthetics, logic and epistemology have remained within the field of philosophy proper. The question is now whether these last philosophical disciplines, especially ethics, may develop into moral science the way natural philosophy has developed into natural science.

The philosophers who, starting with the Renaissance, designed the natural sciences did so in two ways: one, by developing a powerful intellectual tool to serve as the guide for their experiments and deductions, namely the pure science of mathematics; and, two, by establishing frames of reference for each realm of phenomena and confining their inquiry to the particular frame of reference in question. These philosophers saw that the book of nature was written in the symbols of mathematics, except that in their time mathematics existed only rudimentally and had to be developed as their tool as they went along. Gradually, pure and applied mathematics separated. The pure mathematician further elaborated the science and, on the simple foundation of a few basic axioms, erected the modern structure of mathematics, from arithmetic, algebra and analysis up to non-Euclidean geometries, matrices, topology, and similar creations. In this way, mathematics became a pattern for all kinds of possible frames of reference from which applied scientists borrowed freely, fitting their observations into appropriate mathematical frames. Thus astronomy used the calculus, differential and integral equations, and later non-Euclidean spaces; electrical theory used the science of complex numbers; quantum theory borrowed the matrix calculus; thermodynamics, the calculus of probability. This meant, and this was the second important facet in the development of the natural sciences, that each frame of reference had its own laws and significance. Natural philosophy split up into physics, chemistry, biology, astronomy, etc., and these sciences again into sub-sciences, each precisely defined, with its own frame of reference and its own set of phenomena. Yet, different as all these sciences were from one another, they all partook of the formal superstructure of mathematics.

If we want to construct moral science in a similar way we ought to design a superstructure which is to the moral sciences as mathematics is to the natural sciences. It ought to be formal and universal, built on simple axioms, and contain all possible frames of reference for the moral sciences. Such a system would be the logic of these sciences, just as mathematics is the logic of the natural sciences. This system, in turn, would define the moral sciences and their content.

There are two ways in which philosophers have tried to bring about this new science, the naturalistic and non-naturalistic. They have tried either to use the apparatus of the natural sciences, the mathematical and empirical method, or to develop an entirely new method which has nothing to do with that of natural science but is original to moral science.

The former approach was made by the founders of natural science themselves. Descartes, the inventor of analytic geometry, intended not only a mathematical natural science but also such a moral science. Like natural science it was to be based on the *mathesis universalis*, which today we call logic:

> Most of all was I delighted with Mathematics because of the certainty of its demonstrations

and the evidence of its reasoning, but I did not yet understand its true use, and, believing that it was of service only in the mechanical arts, I was astonished that, seeing how firm and solid was its basis, no loftier edifice had been reared there-upon. On the other hand I compared the works of the ancient pagans which deal with Morals to palaces most superb and magnificent, which are yet built on sand and mud alone. They praise the virtues most highly and show them to be more worthy of being prized than anything else in the world, but they do not sufficiently teach us to become acquainted with them, and often that which is called by a fine name is nothing but insensibility, or pride, or despair, or parricide.

Descartes projected his own method as a generaliza-tion of mathematics, containing "everything which gives certainty to the rules of Arithmetic," and "in making use of it" he felt that his "mind gradually accustomed itself to conceive of its objects more accurately and distinctly; and not having restricted this Method to any particular matter," he promised himself "to apply it as usefully to the difficulties of other sciences as I had done to those of Algebra." Descartes' goal was not only to reformulate a natural science, but also a "mathematical morality": that was the bold program! Nothing in the development and the system of Descartes can be rightly understood unless this is understood. For Leibniz, the differential calculus was only part of a large calculus of universal logic applicable to all the sciences and humanities, so that "two philosophers who disagreed about a particular point instead of arguing fruitlessly would take out their pencils and calculate." As for Descartes and Leibniz, so for the other philosophers of that great age: the science of morality was based on the method of natural science. Spinoza applied the geometrical method to the whole of ethics in an *ethica ordine geometrico demonstrata.* Locke wrote his *Essay* as prolegomena to "a subject very remote from this," namely morality and revealed religion, and showed "that moral knowledge is as capable of real certainty as mathematics." The full title of Hume's Treatise is *A Treatise on Human Nature, Being an Attempt to Introduce the Experimental Method of Reasoning into Moral Subjects.* And even Berkeley used epistemology only as a tool for theological ethics, the rules of which "have the same immutable universal truth with the proportions of geometry."

Thus, the greatest philosophers of the modern age have attempted to found a science of ethics on the method of natural science—and failed. The reason is that the world of value is of such a nature that mathematical and empirical methods cannot be applied to it. If they are, ethics turns into a natural science, such as psychology or sociology, and disappears. Ethics is a very elusive game; unless it is approached just right it will change in our hands and vanish—like the princess of the fairy tale who when "caught" appeared as a deer.

This autonomous nature of ethics was already seen by Plato, but the philosopher who established it in modern times is Immanuel Kant. From him dates the non-naturalistic tradition, which culminated in 1903 in the English philosopher G. E. Moore. For Kant, the metaphysics of morals was to applied ethics as pure mathematics is to applied mathematics; so that applied ethics would be in the field of moral philosophy what applied mathematics, or natural science, is in the field of natural philosophy. The principle of this systematic or scientific ethics were developed by Kant in opposition to the empirical, though not in opposition to the formal principles of natural science; even though the formality of ethics is of a different kind from that of natural science.

Kant had a good foundation for his dichotomy between natural and moral cognition. The knowledge of value is fundamentally different from the knowledge of fact for the simple reason that values are fundamentally different from facts. They cannot be observed by the senses or measured by meter rods or weighed by scales. Yet there is no doubt among most men—except radical logical positivists—that we do value and that value judgments, such as "Cheating is wrong," do mean something. The question then is, what do they mean? And, even more fundamentally, what does it mean that they do? What kind of meaning do they have? Do they refer to anything, such as a realm of values, or do they refer to nothing? If the latter, what kind of meaning could they possibly have? Are they merely noises made by people to express their attitudes of like and dislike, and thus subject to psychology rather than philosophy, as are dream symbols and psychosomatic expressions like hiccups or ejaculations? Are they functions of situations and hence belong to sociology and anthropology, like magic formulae and ceremonial utterances? Or are they the kind of non-referential statements like those of mathematics or logic which, although they refer to nothing, are yet applicable to everything—as was the notion of Plato and Locke but not of Kant? All these views have been held and are being held, with the first (the ontological view of value realms) prevalent on the continents of Europe, Latin America and Asia; the second (the view that value judgments are psychological or situational manifestations) prevalent in England and the United States; and the third view maintained by individual thinkers in Europe and in America.

The reason for this confusing variety of views on value is, of course, that nobody really knows what values are. If they were part of the sensory world, natural science would account for them. Some philosophers solve the problem simply by saying that they are and that natural science does account for them, but others are equally convinced that they are not and that natural science does not apply to them. This, however, does not necessarily mean that no science applies to them. Numbers are not of the sensory world either, yet nobody would hold that when we say "a0 = 1" we merely express an emotion or magic formula. What we express is a formula of mathematics. The trouble with axiology is that we do not yet have a system within which value judgments find their place, as mathematical judgments do in mathematics. When there is no system there is confusion; and for this reason value judgments are open to a free-for-all, with some announcing they refer to something, others that they refer to nothing, and again others that they express psychological or sociological states. Thus values have the usual epistemological status of things unknown, no more nor less than, say, flying saucers. Some believe there are, some that there are not, and some that they are merely hallucinations. So with value. Some believe there are values, some that there are not, and some that they are merely hallucinations. Or, if we go back to historical precedents, values have the same epistemological status today as had the Stone of the Wise, the Fountain of Youth, or Phlogiston, the Principle of Fire. Some said these existed and some they did not, and C. G. Jung has shown that they were merely symbols of the unconscious mind.

The one way to break the magic circle of which these and other pre-scientific images were part was to break completely with the entire world picture they represented and make a new and original beginning. This, in natural science, was the historical accomplishment of Galileo. He invented an entirely new frame of reference in which to think of heaven and earth: the mathematical. His simple formulae opened up—by reason, not by magic persuasion—the storehouse of nature from which we have drawn the energy of the modern age.

Thus our present confusion about value is nothing new or unique. In attacking a problem, say, to find X, there are three, and only three, logical possibilities: (1) to say there is no X, and that ends the problem right there; (2) to say there is X, and then to start looking both for it and for ways of looking for it; or (3) the intermediate position of saying there is and there is not X; there is in one sense and there is not in another. The first position is "No, there is no value;" the second, "Yes, there is value:" the third, "Yes, there is value, but—or No, there is no value, but—." The first is the non-cognitivist position, the second the cognitivist, and the third the semi-cognitivist, or semi-non-cognitivist position. All three have today their significant representatives whose views range from the non-existence and non-knowability of values to their existence and exact knowability.

If we take the ultimate logical comprehension of value as a goal toward which value theory ought to strive, we get a spectrum reaching from those that deny all possibility of value knowledge to those who not only affirm such a possibility but design actual systems. The latter approach the problem on the basis of five propositions, each of which is denied by one or another axiological school, namely, (1) There is value; (2) Value is knowable; (3) Value knowledge consists in systematization; (4) Systematization is based on axiomatic formulation and deductive expansion of the essence of the value experiences; (5) The value system proves itself by the scope of its applicability to the value world.

This is the scientific position we are taking.

We conceive of a theory of values analogous to a science which, from a minimum of axiomatic assumptions derives a multitude of conclusions, in a pattern so varied and detailed that its features correspond to the multitude of features found in value reality.

The theory of value, therefore, is conceived as a pattern isomorphous with the sphere of value. The structure of value is the structure of the pattern pertaining to and explanatory of this sphere. This conception presupposes that there are value phenomena, that these phenomena can be ordered, and that this order can be reflected in a theoretical structure: the theory of value or axiology. Thus, value appears on three levels: that of the axiological pattern, formal value; that of the sphere of value, phenomenal value; and that of the combination of the two, axiological value. These three levels combine to form the Science of Value. The conception of such a science presupposes several distinctions which have never been clearly made. In natural science they did not have to be made because they were obvious. But they have to be made explicitly in moral philosophy, where they are anything but obvious.

Failure to make the distinctions in question has been one of the main obstacles, if not the main obstacle, to the development of a science of value and, indeed, of orderly thinking in the value field.

A botanist who dissects a rose does not run the risk, neither does he suffer the temptation, of thinking that he smells like a rose, or that, in dissecting the rose he is dissecting himself. The botanist cannot possibly confuse himself with the subject matter of his discipline. A psychologist is in a more precarious situation in this respect. He has to identify himself with his patient, and it is not impossible, theoretically at least, that he might go so far as to confuse himself with the patient. Needless to say, if this identification were complete and caused the psychologist the total loss of his rational detachment, his usefulness as an analyst would come to an end and he himself would be transformed into a patient.

The theoreticians of value have considered their situation more analogous to that of the psychologist than that of the botanist. Instead of recognizing the danger of identifying themselves with their subject matter to the point of losing their rational detachment, they have made such loss of detachment, vaguely, a condition of their axiological activity. Actually, no systematic investigation has been made so far into the relationship between the theory of value and its subject matter, value.

Consequently, this relationship has remained in the dark. In particular, the danger of losing one's own efficacy as a theoretician of value on becoming involved in valuing, has not been examined or even recognized. As a result, the theory of value and its subject matter, value, are constantly being confused: valuers believe they are analyzing value, and value analysts believe they are valuing; philosophers of value believe they should be involved, committed, etc., and valuers who are involved, committed, etc. believe they should philosophize. Thus, philosophy and value, value and ideology, commitment and reasoning are today all mixed up. The resulting confusion not only plays havoc with moral philosophy in our time but also with social and political "science" and the humanities in general.

The fundamental distinction in question is the self-evident one between thought and the object of thought. This implies the following distinctions: between thought and action, between form and content, between subject matter and method, between theory and practice, between meaning and usage, between knowing-that and knowing-how. These distinctions, in turn, determine those between order and disorder, clarity and confusion, coherence and fragmentation, relevance and triviality. In other words, the fundamental distinction between thought and its object is the condition *sine qua non* for the order, clarity, coherence and relevance of a theory, while the fusion of thought with its object leads, in differing degrees, to the disorder, confusion, fragmentation and triviality of a theory. All this, of course, is too obvious for natural science and traditional philosophy even to be mentioned. But for value theory this clarification is important, for a great part of value theory is based on the confusion in question.

As a result, the three levels of value—formal value, phenomenal value, and the combination of both, axiological value—are not distinguished. This simply means that value has not been made the object of orderly thinking. Value is, in reality, not the subject of a theory, and the denomination "theory" of value is a euphemism.

For us, value is as much an object of knowledge as any other, no different in this respect from the rose for the botanist, or electric current for the physicist. The botanist, as we said, does not exude a rosy aroma and the physicist does not give off sparks. By the same token, the axiologist does not value, he analyzes value. When the botanist gives his sweetheart a rose, or when the physicist takes the bread out of the toaster, they are not operating as either botanist or physicist. They are operating simply as human beings in everyday situations. These situations incidentally exemplify certain characteristics of their professional callings; but as a botanist and as a physicist, their respective tasks do not consist in giving roses to sweethearts or taking bread out of toasters. Their respective tasks consist in being professionals and experts in roses and electric currents, that is to say, in being familiar with the fundamental principles and general laws which serve as the bases for all valuing.

Axiology, then, is for those who want to be experts or professionals in value, or for those who want to know about value as do (or as ought to do) the experts and professionals. Axiology is to value what pulmonary physiology is to respiration. The lung specialist is neither a yogi nor a fakir specializing in respiratory exercises; as a specialist, he is not committed to any particular way of life that contains respiratory exercises; he breathes like everyone else. When he breathes, he is not a specialist in respiration. On the contrary, if there is something wrong with his respiration, he will probably consult a colleague. The specialist in value is neither a saint nor a devil specializing in valuational exercises; as a specialist he is not committed to any particular way of life and the valuational exercises that are a part of it; he values like everyone else. When he values he is not a specialist in valuation. And it is entirely likely that when the science of valuation achieves the development comparable to that of medicine, the axiologist might consult a colleague if something goes wrong with his valuation.

Axiology, then, does not offer exercises in valuation but the principle of value.

The botanist has no fear that his work will interfere with his enjoyment of roses, nor does the physicist fear that his knowledge of currents will interfere with his enjoyment of the benefits of toasters, nor is the lung specialist afraid this his physiological knowledge of lungs will interfere with his breathing. The tale of the centipede, who, on being asked which leg he used first, lost the use of all of them, is, therefore, apocryphal. The same occurs in the matter of valuation. The expert in value does not relinquish his enjoyment of the experience of value by knowing the principles of value. On the contrary, it might be said that his enjoyment is greater, in a way more subtle, just as the knowledge of the botanist, the electrical physicist or the lung specialist adds a certain subtle hue, a piquant new dimension to their human activities—a fact exploited by the hostess who asked a famous surgeon to carve the turkey. In general, theoretical knowledge of a field does not destroy the human involvement in this field; rather it intensifies it through rational penetration. To think otherwise is fundamentally to misunderstand the use of human reason. The distinction between thought and its object does not separate the two; on the contrary it fuses them. For thought cannot be thought unless it is distinct from its object and only then can it penetrate its object. Thought must be opposed to action in order to fuse with it. Fusing the two without distinction is confusion. Such confusion is that of the dilettante and distinguishes him from the expert. The musical dilettante enjoys music but does not know the score. The musical expert knows the score. This does not destroy his enjoyment of the symphony but heightens it. His musical sensibility is rationally structured. Axiological theory is the score of value reality. By it, the sensibility to value is rationally structured.

In the next lecture we shall discuss the laws of harmony that govern this score.

Lecture II

THE CONCEPT OF THE SCIENCE OF VALUE

ABSTRACT

In this second lecture, Hartman defines those elements that constitute "science." He distinguishes science in general from particular sciences. Science, in general, is thought pattern applied to a set of objects. Science as a frame of reference ought not to be confused with content, although it often is. Hartman explains why logic and content are different, how they are often confused, and he describes the unfortunate consequences of such confusion. Step-by-step, he describes the assorted fallacies that give rise to this confusion, illustrating his points with examples from Jesus, Marx, Lavoisier, as well as numerous philosophers and scientists over the centuries. By the conclusion of this lecture, he has established the moral groundwork for a science of value, which he begins to define in Lecture Three.

Through the centuries, the difficulties encountered by philosophers from Plato to Dilthey and Dewey, in trying to establish a science of value, have arisen, primarily out of the uncertainty of the concept of science itself. What is a science? And what can be a science of value? The question begins as far back as Plato, continues with Aristotle, the Stoics, the Neo-Platonists, the medieval philosophers—St. Augustine, St. Anselm, St. Thomas—and persists with great intellectual and spiritual vigor among the modern philosophers from the Renaissance on, who took natural science as their model for the construction of a Science of Value.

As we saw in the first lecture, these philosophers, the greatest in modern history, and their successors in recent and contemporary philosophy, have not succeeded in developing the science of value, the moral science, which they considered not only possible but necessary. They failed for the simple reason that they did not have an accurate knowledge of the concept of science itself. They believed that either the formal pattern—mathematics— or the empirical method—experiment, observation, prediction—of natural science, could be applied intact, without any modification, to the field of morality. In this way, they committed methodological fallacies which we are aware of today, because we have analyzed the concept of science in general.

Science in general is neither natural nor moral science, but simply science. That is, science is a method which has nothing to do with the content, the object or subject matter of the science. The subject matter of specific sciences gives to science in general specific differentia: the subject matter of nature gives the sciences dealing with this subject the specific character of natural sciences; the subject matter of music gives the corresponding science the characteristic of musical science or harmony; and the subject matter of morality, or value in general, gives the science dealing with this subject the specific character of valuational science or axiology. There is possible, then, an infinity of specific sciences. Science in general is that which all these particular sciences have in common: It is a thought pattern applied to a set of objects. In a developed science, the thought pattern is always a systematic structure, a logic or formal system, logic being the form of the structure of thought. Thus, the pattern for natural science is mathematics, the pattern for the science of music is harmonic theory, and the pattern for the science of value is formal axiology.

The consideration of such a pattern is nothing new. It goes back to Plato who, in his theory of ideas, his dialectic science, noesis and dianoia, planned a science of science and, in his last book, *The Laws*, even planned an Institute for it, called the Nocturnal Council, whose members had to "understand the laws that control the stars," astronomy and mathematics, to relate them to musical theory, and "to apply all of this harmonically to the institutions and rules of ethics."

But the elaboration of this science presupposes a requirement that neither Plato nor any other of the philosophers mentioned possessed, namely, an exact knowledge of the nature of a pattern or a frame of reference; in particular, of the laws of its axiomatic. As long as the axiomatic nature of a frame of reference remained unknown, it was impossible to know the nature of science. Although the knowledge of axiomatic is still incomplete, gigantic strides have been made in this century, in the works of Hilbert, Russell, Whitehead, Gödel, and others. Since 1910 in particular, when Russell and Whitehead began to publish their *Principia Mathematica*, the formally logical nature of the frame of reference of natural science, mathematics, has been demonstrated, and the fundamental concept of mathematics, number, defined in strictly logical terms. "I call," says Russell, "mathematical logic any work which has as its end the analysis and deduction of arithmetic, as well as geometry, by means of concepts which belong ostensibly to logic." Paraphrasing Russell, we say that, "We call axiological any work which has as its end the analysis and deduction of ethics, as well as the other moral sciences, by means of concepts which ostensibly belong to logic."

The task consists then in defining the fundamental concept of axiology, "value," in strictly logical terms. Once this is done, the science of formal axiology can be erected on the foundation of this definition, thus creating an intellectual instrument which would function with relation to the natural sciences, or as harmonic theory functions with relation to music: as a frame of reference which precisely defines these sciences, formulates their terms, and makes them applicable to the realities of social and moral life. By this means the moral, aesthetic, metaphysical, religious, political, sociological and other phenomena and situations which, until now, have been vaguely perceived, ill-defined and, therefore, badly comprehended, would become the objects of an exact science. Due to the lack of such a science, man, with all his good will, has not been able to realize this good will, for he has never been able to see clearly what it was he was to realize.

Most people do not have bad will but faulty knowledge. I understood this when I was a young man in Germany, and I understand it today: if the Germans had known how evil Hitler was, "the incarnation of evil in history" as a German Ambassador said recently, they would not have voted for him. They did not have sufficient knowledge to recognize in the innocent beginnings of the Nazi movement the germ of the monstrous evil that was to follow. They did not have an accurate science to show them. This conviction of my youth led me to the present studies in axiology.

Before presenting an outline of the science of axiology, I should like to mention several of the consequences that follow from the mere conception of such a science, from the mere assumption that it might be possible. The science of axiology should have, and does have two principal tasks: (a) the negative one of analysis or criticism of the traditional moral disciplines, and (b) the positive one of synthesis or construction of such new sciences. The first task presupposes an analytical instrument for criticism. The second presupposes an exact system to define, in its own terms, the concepts of the moral sciences. The first task is accomplished by the so-called axiological fallacies and the notion of method, which arise from the mere concept of an axiological science, in a simple manner. The second task is accomplished by the axiological system itself which defines, in its own terms, the fundamental concepts and relationships of the moral sciences. We shall, in this lecture which deals with the concept of axiological science, discuss the methodological and axiological fallacies and in the next lecture which deals with the science itself, the construction of the new science.

From the concepts of a science as the combination of a formal pattern with a set of objects or phenomena, it follows that each science has its own frame of reference and, consequently, its own set of phenomena. That is, a datum becomes an object of natural science if the frame of natural science is applied to it. An airplane that drops an atom bomb on a city is an object of natural science or, as we can also say, a fact, when it is studied in the light of the sciences of navigation aerodynamics, physics, mechanics, etc. But it is transformed into an object of axiological science, a value, when examined in the light of moral science. The observation made in his navigation log by the co-pilot of the Enola Gay, the plane that dropped the atomic bomb on Hiroshima, when he saw a whole city disappear: "My God, what have we done!" is not an object of natural science but of moral science.

The same datum may, then, appear either as an object of natural science or of moral science depending on the point of view, or on the pattern applied. Thus the world, which is ontologically one, can appear in as many aspects as there are frames of reference applied to it; in the same way as, for example, the same curve can appear convex or concave, straight or curved, depending on the viewpoint adopted (in the differential calculus it appears straight).

If it is true that each science has its own frame of reference and its own set of phenomena, then there follows an important conclusion: it is fallacious from the point of view of science, to confuse either the frames of reference, or the sets of phenomena, or both, of different sciences. Such confusions constitute the axiological fallacies. When the mathematical frame of reference is confused with the axiological frame of reference, that is, the natural point of view is confused with the moral, there results what we call the metaphysical fallacy, a metaphysical view of the world that is fallacious. This fallacy is committed by those who believe they can reach conclusions about the world of nature based on the world of value, or vice versa. This fallacy can be found in abundance: in the arguments of the Church against Galileo and in those of the atheists against the Church; in the writings of modern physicists, such as Jeans or Eddington, on value, and those of ethicists on nature, as in the arguments that the principle of indeterminacy in quantum physics demonstrates man's free will, or that the theory of relativity demonstrates the ideality of the world. This fallacy also appears in the writings of the modern philosophers mentioned in the first lecture.

The knowledge of this fallacy already brings a certain order into the confused arguments of today and yesterday.

The second fallacy has similar scope. Not only can the general frames of reference of the natural and axiological sciences be confused, but also the specific frames of reference of particular natural and axiological sciences. The confusion among the various natural sciences is no longer possible due to the existence of the mathematical frame of reference which orders these sciences; but it was quite common before the modern age. Thus, music and astronomy were confused by Pythagoras and even by Kepler; theology and astronomy by Aristotle and even by Newton; theology and chemistry by the alchemists. Today we still lack knowledge of the frames of reference of the specific axiological sciences, hence confusions between these sciences is not only common but usual. Ethics and psychology are confused when it is stated that good is pleasure; ethics and theology when it is said that good is the will of God; ethics and economy, when the good is made dependent on economic systems as in Marxism; ethics and sociology when ethics is regarded a matter of society; ethics and aesthetics when the good is "converted" into the beautiful, and so on. This fallacy, of confusing specific axiological sciences with one another or with natural sciences is called the naturalistic fallacy because a non-naturalistic ethical good is usually confused with a naturalistic good.

Not only can the general or the specific frames of reference be confused, but also the general with the specific ones. This no longer happens very often in natural science, where it would consist of a confusion between mathematics, on the one hand, and physics or chemistry, on the other; even though this does still happen, for example in popular writings on science in which formulae are "translated" into ordinary language. But it was a common confusion before Copernicus and Galileo, as in Plato and Pythagoras, who confused elements of number with elements of nature. In moral thinking this fallacy means a confusion of value in general with a specific value, as in the confusion between goodness in general with moral goodness. To say that a murderer cannot be good is to commit this fallacy. A murderer cannot be morally good, but he may be good as a murderer, that is, he may kill well. This fallacy we call the moral fallacy because its most common instances are the confusion of good in general with moral good. It was Plato who clearly recognized this fallacy; all of his works are an effort towards separating Goodness from Being, on the one hand, thus avoiding the metaphysical fallacy, and from specific goods on the other hand, thus avoiding the moral fallacy (especially, in the Socratic dialogues).

Finally, there is possible a confusion between the specific frame of reference and the subject matter of a particular science. This we call the fallacy of method. In the natural sciences this fallacy is quite rare in one sense, and quite usual in another. It is rare in the sense that a scientist rarely confuses himself with his subject matter, for example, an electronics scientist with an electron. Nevertheless, it is necessary to specify this relationship, and this has been done with mathematical precision in Heisenberg's indeterminacy principle. Also, this relationship between the scientist and his subject matter is important in the philosophy of operationism of Bridgman, and in the construction of the observer in relativity theory. This relationship, then, is clearly defined in today's science. But this was not true in the Middle Ages, when the scientist was confused with his subject matter, as occurred in alchemy, where certain personal commitments were necessary in order to produce a chemical effect.

In another sense, this fallacy is quite common today in natural science. Frequently natural science is confused with its subject matter in the sense that certain properties of the subject matter are taken for properties of the science itself. Thus, it is said that science is empirical and that for this reason an axiological science is impossible since it neither predicts nor observes, or else, if it were possible, it should be empirical, that is, it should predict and observe. Let us call this species of fallacy of method the empirical fallacy. It could also be considered a type of metaphysical fallacy because it confuses science in general with natural science, as occurs in the commission of the metaphysical fallacy in which natural science is taken as science in general, including moral science.

As we said at the start, what makes a science is its method, not its content. If there exists a formal systematic pattern applicable to a set of objects, then there exists a science, regardless of the nature of its subject matter, which might be spatio-temporal and hence observable and predictable, or not. Thus, mathematics, music, and axiology are as much sciences as natural science; and their contents are observable and predictable, for these two characteristics are nothing more than the result of the application of a frame of reference and the conformity of phenomena to this frame of reference. In music, the note Heifetz will play next in a given concerto can be predicted from the score, which is the frame of reference; in mathematics, the mathematical result of a specific operation can be predicted; and the same occurs in the case of axiology. Given a certain situation and applying the axiological frame of reference to it, the axiological result can be predicted. It happens to be a peculiarity of natural science that its formal prediction coincides with a temporal process of its objects; and this material process is confused with the formal predictability of any science as such. What makes this confusion particularly serious is the fact that the temporal process which is the subject of natural science, is not temporal in the sense of having past, present and future, but that it is itself formal, being nothing more than the counterpart of a linear geometric relation. The empirical fallacy, then, is a confusion of thought that goes to the very core of natural science.

In the moral field, the fallacy of method appears with extraordinary frequency with good reason, for in this area there is not, as yet, a formal frame of reference. So it is maintained, as for instance by Hume, that ethics does not lend itself to rational treatment because the moral sense is not rational—an argument also popular with the so-called logical positivists. The irrational, in other words, it is held, cannot be subject to rational analysis. If this were true, the psychiatrist should be mad and the cancer specialist would be the one who is sickest with cancer. This fallacy has a multitude of variations: the normative one says that the moral sciences are normative while the natural sciences are not (as we saw in discussing their sanctions, the moral sciences are no more nor less normative than the natural sciences); and the existentialist variation states that the philosopher can explain human life only through his own being human, and this being human not in general but in his own individual selfhood.

According to the conception of science we have developed, there is a difference between a science and its subject-matter. Because this essential difference remained unclarified, partly through neglect and partly through a determined effort to becloud it—on the part of philosophers such as the *Geistewissenschaftler*, of the type of Dilthey, and certain philosophical anthropologists such as Heidegger—the axiological sciences have remained in a backward stage of development. To make the distinction between subject and object in a moral science is, it is true, quite difficult, but it must be made if one wants to analyze and know. Being is one thing and to analyze Being is another. Just as a policeman can arrest himself or a judge can fine himself—for, although ontologically one they can act in different functions—so a scientific axiologist, in order to carry out his function, must put aside his being for his knowing, even though knowing he is and being he knows. But he does not know ontologically but epistemologically, and he is not epistemologically but ontologically. At bottom, the existentialist species of the fallacy of method is the naturalistic fallacy, which confuses two distinct axiological sciences, ontology and epistemology.

The axiological fallacies arise out of the mere conception of an axiological science as a powerful instrument of intellectual analysis. Out of this same conception arises the concept of method. The difference between philosophy and science is that philosophy has no method while science has. Or more accurately, the method of science is effective while the method of philosophy is ineffective. The method of chemical science is effective while the method of chemical philosophy, alchemy, was ineffective. Since today we have moral philosophy and lack moral science we have an ineffective moral method and lack an effective one. We are living in an age of social alchemy, and this is true of all current social theories from the so-called right to the so-called left.

The reason for the effectiveness of science and the in-effectiveness of philosophy lies in the difference between the types of concepts employed by these two disciplines. Philosophical concepts become less precise in the degree to which they become more general, and scientific concepts become more precise in the degree to which they become more general. Philosophical concepts are abstract, scientific concepts are formal. The distinction between abstraction and formalism has been elaborated in the past by Kant and the present by Husserl. Abstract concepts are "drawn off," "abstracted" from the empirical world, formal concepts are constructed by means of axioms. Being abstracted from concrete reality, the former, the concepts of philosophy, are material; and their meaning becomes more and more vague the farther removed they are from their original source. In the end they mean practically nothing, such as the philosophical concept of Being or the philosophical concept of Value. On the other hand, the formal or axiomatic concepts used by science, not being abstracted from concrete reality but constructed by creative human minds such as Galileo or Einstein, do not become vague in the degree of their generality. On the contrary, as they grow more general in extension, they grow more meaningful in intension. Their meaning becomes more and more precise, until they cover vast realms of phenomena, such as, for example, the scientific concept of matter or the scientific concept of value. The systematic power of formal concepts lies in their being deduced from axioms. An axiom is the formulation, by means of a mathematical or logical formula, of the essence of a vast group of phenomena; and it is the art of the creative scientist to discover these formulations, as did Einstein in the set of formulae which include the famous formula $E = mc^2$, which in five symbols gives us the essence of atomic energy with the resulting nuclear bombs and future planetary travel.

The power of the system of mathematics, as of any genuine system, lies, then, in the axiomatic formalism of the system. The more formal mathematics is, the more precise and general is its application. On the other hand, the more abstract philosophy is, the less precise and general is its application. For this reason it is said of the philosopher that he knows less and less of more and more until, in the end, he knows nothing about everything, while of the scientist that he knows more and more about less and less until, in the end, he knows everything about nothing. But his nothing of which the scientist knows everything is not simply zero as the limit of everything. And so, science really knows everything about everything that can be formulated in axiomatic form. It is for this reason that scientific knowledge is more effective than the ineffective knowledge of philosophy.

It is clear, then, that if we truly want to know what value is, we must know scientifically and must stop knowing philosophically.

The application of a formal system or science produces a world ordered by precise relations, that is, by the relations of the system in question, while the application of a vague system or philosophy produces a world that is disordered for the lack of such relations. The application of the natural sciences produced our technological world while the application of philosophy produced the world of alchemy and astrology of the Middle Ages, and our present moral world.

The problem of how to produce a moral world, then, can be solved simply and logically: the moral world is a constitutive part of moral science, and moral science is a constitutive part of the moral world. Moral science is the theoretical part of the moral world, and the moral world is the practical part of moral science. Without moral science there is no moral world, and without a moral world there is no moral science. Thus, the creation of a moral science already constitutes the first step towards a moral world. This fact answers the question of why, if the Christian and other religions have been preaching for centuries that all men should love each other, no world of fraternal love has yet resulted. This preachment has been and still is ineffectual because it has not been based on a necessity of human thinking, and hence of human action. Or, in more precise terms, because goodness has remained, until now, a philosophical and not a scientific concept. The history of science and technology has proved the basic justness and accuracy of the Socratic thesis that man will do what he knows, if by "knowing" is meant scientific knowing in the sense defined.

Therefore, there exists no difference between the active and practically productive nature of natural science and that of moral science; and the characterization of ethics as the only doctrine of action is fundamentally wrong. Any science will bring about a corresponding action, be it natural or moral or musical or whatever other kind. The concept of science, as we have said, implies that of method.

The cause for the lack of morality in the world can now be determined exactly: it is the lack of a moral science in the strictly defined sense, the lack of scientific and truly formal moral concepts. What we have is a pre-scientific Ethics. Its philosophical concepts render ineffectual ethical thinking, in spite of all the good will in the world—just as the same type of thinking in natural philosophy rendered ineffectual natural thinking, in spite of all the good will of people to fly through the air, penetrate into the earth, ride over the seas, or to see or hear beyond the horizon or within their own veins and arteries. At one time, all these things belonged to the realm of dreams and utopias, neither more nor less dreamy or utopian than today's desires of a moral world. The mathematico-empirical method has transformed these dreams into realities; and there is nothing to keep the axiological-moral method from transforming into realities the dreams of our time.

The knowledge of Good can be historically effective or ineffective depending on whether it is scientific or philosophic. Effective knowledge, until now, has been either the scientific knowledge of nature or the pseudo-scientific knowledge of society. Neither has ever led to moral good, the first, because the knowledge of nature is morally neutral and can be used for good as well as evil; the second, because the knowledge of society was pseudo-scientific rather than scientific, comprised of abstracted rather than formal concepts, whose implicative connections, moreover, were inflated to gigantic proportions, transforming these concepts into absolute metaphysical truths which falsified morality and distorted moral and social thinking.

Jesus Christ himself understood this apparent lack of method in his teachings and prophesied an era in which they would not be understood and heeded and another in which they would be understood and heeded; an era in which all that he had taught would be taught anew and he would again be remembered (John 14:26). We interpret this in the sense that the teachings of Christ must be re-taught, not as philosophical and abstract precepts devoid of precise meaning, but as axiologically scientific and axiomatic concepts with precise meaning: as effective, not ineffective knowledge. Instead of analyzing the Gospel as inefficient in the past, which is obvious to anyone, we should develop intellectual instruments to make it effective for the future.

Examples of morally inefficient words ("freedom") and actions (e.g. war) are too abundant to mention (e.g. the war in Vietnam in the name of "freedom"). All we have to do is sharpen our mind and sight to recognize them and to recognize the reason for their inefficiency: in each case, lack of definition, vagueness, abstract and philosophical expression, instead of precision exactness, formal and scientific expression.

There is little doubt that natural science has transformed the world from the medieval village into the technological colossi of today and that, currently, thanks to natural science, we are on the verge of either extinction or undreamed-of abundance. There is no doubt, also, that a social theory such as Marxism has transformed the world. But, curiously, this transformation is not as original as that produced by technological science. Marxism is, rather, the servant of this science; and the fact that it is, and that it is to a greater degree than capitalism, is one of those sources of Marxist pride. The problem then is: what is the common denominator by means of which both natural science and Marxism have effected their transformation of the world; and, in particular, where is the point at which the valuational functions of Marxism and of natural science are distinguished?

As we have already seen, natural science has a triple structure consisting of three levels:

(1) The formal science of mathematics

(2) Theoretical and applied science

(3) The scientific phenomena.

This structure has been effective and has led to the transformation of society, because the phenomena of science follow the frame of reference not only logically but also chronologically: as a result of the new theoretical comprehension of the world actually a new world was developed, almost organically, through the natural functioning of the human mind. The mind acts as soon as it comprehends; as soon as it comprehends in a new way, it acts in a new way, and it transforms the world. Knowledge, in this sense, is power, as Bacon declared. Effective knowledge, then, for good or for bad, is systematic formal knowledge.

The effectiveness of such knowledge can also be found, to some degree, in the social science of Karl Marx. In Karl Marx we can readily see the transition from pre-scientific knowledge to scientific knowledge, although here "scientific" means something quite different from what it means in natural science. The general structure of so-called Marxist science is the same as that of natural science, consisting of a superstructure, the theoretical and applied sciences, and the phenomena. But the superstructure has a characteristic difference from that of natural science: its relations are not formal but abstract, not deductions from axioms but abstractions from sense reality. The Hegelian logic, therefore, is philosophy rather than science, and so is Marxism. Its relations are implicative and material: the terms of each triad do not arise out of the formal logic of the system as such, but from the abstract meaning of the concepts in question. One must know what the concept serving as thesis means in order to produce both the antithesis and the synthesis; and this production is as uncertain and arbitrary as all conceptual implications (as the grotesque failure of Hegel's natural philosophy proves). Moreover, Hegelian as well as Marxian logic confuses contrariety with contradiction. Hegel's social philosophy and its Marxist inversion seem to be more plausible and effective than other social theories only because there is no standard by which they could be checked, as exists in natural science.

Consequently, Marxism as a social theory suffers from the same pseudo-scientific character as the rest of social theories, although in a less obvious way due to the pseudo-formalism of its Hegelian superstructure and the corresponding pseudo-empiricism of its economic substructure. It is effective for lack of something better. Compared with the majority of social philosophies today and their analytic concepts, Marxism has a point in its conviction that it possesses a "scientific" instrument with which to comprehend and transform the world. But compared with a genuine science based on formal axiomatic concepts, this conviction is erroneous. In terms of such a science, the structure of the Marxist so-called "science" is only apparently scientific.

Marx was very acute in his criticism of capitalism but very vague in his vision of Communism. In fact, he wrote almost nothing on Communism, and Lenin had to experiment on a day to day basis. Marx was astute in the first task of science, criticism, but failed in the second, construction. He lacked a truly axiomatic system.

Today, the Marxist period of superiority over the social philosophies is rapidly coming to an end. The econometric methods of von Neumann, Leontief, and other pioneers of the mathematics of economic systems, are opening up new perspectives which render obsolete the prescientific notions on which both capitalism and communism are based. In the course of this generation, both economic systems will appear as simply two among an infinity of mathematical possibilities of optimizing economic processes. Thus, today's struggle will join other once mortal conflicts in the mausoleum of history.

No economic system is, merely by virtue of its being an economic system, at the same time a moral system. It might be a moral system but it might also be immoral or amoral. Morality is one thing, economics is another. And, as we shall see, morality holds the primacy in value. Both economic systems, the capitalist and Marxist, fail economically precisely where they fail morally. Economic efficiency depends on moral efficiency.

What is needed, then, is knowledge of moral efficiency; knowledge that is, at once, morally good and socially efficient. Following what we have said, this knowledge can only be axiomatic knowledge of good. This means that the nature of good itself must be investigated with systematic precision. However, the nature of good is not the nature of things that are good. Therefore, what must be investigated with systematic precision is the concept of "good." To investigate this concept "with systematic precision" means to investigate it as a scientific and not a philosophical concept; a formal, not a material; a logical, not a metaphysical, psychological, sociological, economical, theological, or what not, concept. This means that, as an object of study, there will emerge the scientific term "good" in place of the philosophical concept "good." Moral science, then, should arise from a terminological study of the word "good."

This is the scientific procedure consecrated by time, as a classic of a science as solid and concrete as chemistry will testify, Lavoisier's *Elements of Chemistry*. This science developed from an analysis of chemical language, not from an analysis of chemical compounds—a fact that will seem strange only to those who still have the empirical prejudice. Thus begins this famous work:

> When I began the following work, my only object was to amplify and explain more fully the memorandum I read in the public meeting of the Academy of Science in the month of April, 1787, on the necessity to reform and complete the nomenclature of chemistry. While I was engaged in this work, I perceived better than even before, the truth of the following maxim by the Abbé de Condillac, in his Logic and in some of his other works:

> "We think only through words... Languages are true analytical methods... Algebra, which is adapted to its purpose in every type of expression, in the simplest, most exact and best

possible way, is, at once, a language and an
analytical method… The art of reasoning is
nothing more than a well organized language."

Thus, while I thought I was occupied only with
forming a nomenclature, and while I did not
propose to do more than improve the language
of chemistry, my labors gradually transformed
themselves without my being able to avoid it,
into a treatise on the elements of chemistry.

The same will occur in the case of ethics. The analysis of the language of value will necessarily produce the
elements of a science of axiology. For, again to quote
Lavoisier, "We cannot improve the language of any science without, at the same time, improving the science
itself; and neither can we, on the other hand, improve
a science without improving the language or nomenclature which belongs to it. It does not matter how true
the facts of any science might be and it does not matter
how true are the ideas of these facts that we might have
formed, we can only communicate false impressions to
others while we lack the words with which adequately to
express such facts or ideas."

So we have come full circle: the social efficiency of
moral science depends on its formal elaboration. The
material possibility of such a science depends on its formal possibility.

We must, then, examine the new language of value.

Lecture III

THE AXIOM OF VALUE: WHAT IS GOODNESS?

ABSTRACT

In this third lecture, Hartman describes the core of value. He writes that it is not just a theory, but a method. In this regard, it is like mathematics, and like a musical score. It is a science. What makes it a science is that it is based upon an axiom. He distinguishes science from philosophy by asserting that science is based upon axioms; philosophy is based on categories. He credits G. E. Moore with having discovered the essential axiomatic truth about value. Then, he explains how Moore never was able to complete the line of reasoning that he had started, and concludes by proposing that formal axiology, based on the axiom of "goodness" holds the key to developing a systematic science of value.

So far I have said nothing about precisely what is value but have only presented a few observations based on the conclusions logically derived from the presupposition that value exists and that it can be known by a science. In the first lecture, I presented these conclusions with respect to the concept of value and in the second, the conclusions with respect to the concept of science. I have not spoken of any specific value but of value itself, nor of any specific science but of science itself. Consequently, I have not yet presented a theory of value. I have only offered observations about value and about the science of value, based on the presuppositions mentioned.

Now we will go to the core of value. First of all, we must note that the science of this core, or essence, of value is not just a theory of value in the traditional sense of value philosophies. Rather, it is a method which shows how we think, not how we ought to think, but how we do think when we value. Hence, it is a method which teaches us how to think in valuational terms. It tells us what it means to think or state that something is good or bad; but it does not ask us, or order us, to think that something is good or bad. It is, in this respect, like mathematics which tells us that within its system two and two equals four, but it does not tell us that when we add two and two we must write the total as four. We are entirely free to write the total "five." We write "four" to avoid the resulting confusion and the resulting bankruptcy if we are business men or accountants, or even professors. The sanctions imposed are those of life, not of mathematics. The same occurs in axiology, and in an even higher degree. We can be expert axiologists, knowing with the greatest precision the meaning of good and evil, but does it follow from this that we shall choose good rather than evil? Perhaps, knowing expertly both good and evil, we could, if we so chose, be more evil than any layman. However, this cannot be the case, for the proposition: "X is an expert in axiology and chooses to be evil" is self-contradictory. The expert in axiology knows that evil is a confusion between good and bad, and if he is an expert he cannot possibly choose this confusion. We would have to say: "I know clearly that evil is a confusion, and I choose confusion rather than clarity." This is self-contradictory, as is a mathematician who would use his knowledge to confuse mathematics or a dentist his drill to torture. All this is possible. But then the axiolo-gist is no expert axiologist, the mathematician no expert mathematician, and the dentist no expert dentist. All would have a flaw of character, which would impinge on the clarity, and comprehensiveness of their "knowl-edge." From this follows the converse implication: "If I am an expert axiologist I cannot help but choose the good." This is the old Socratic thesis, and it is axiologi-cally true. For it gives to formal axiology not only the character of a method—"If I choose good, I choose to do good"—but also of a therapy. The more and the more clearly I know formal axiology the more chances I have to correct mistakes in my life and thus to improve myself morally. For the evil person is morally confused. The therapeutic effect of formal axiology has been confirmed by the astonishing diagnostic and therapeutic success of the axiological test that grew out of formal axiology, the Hartman Value Profile.

Still, considering formal axiology as a merely theoret-ical rather than a practical and applied science, it remains true that axiology gives us the meaning of both good and evil but leaves us free to choose one or the other. Should we choose evil, the penalty is analogous to that for math-ematical error: the consequence is confusion and moral bankruptcy. The sanctions imposed are those of life, not of axiology. The situation is the same for all science. We are perfectly free to violate the law of gravity and step out the window, but the result would be breaking our necks. This is a sanction imposed by life, or more accurately, death, but not by the law of gravity.

Formal axiology, thus, is not a theory in the usual sense. It is a method of thinking which one is free to use and, consequently, develop one's own sense of value and one's moral practice, in the same way, as was pointed out in the first lecture, as a score is used to develop one's sense of music. One can decide to use this instrument or not. It all depends on the immediate evidence of the axiological axiom. Only if one feels that this axiom is immediately evident and that it states in symbolic formulation a fact one has always known, only then can and will one use this method. But no matter whether one does or doesn't use it and whether one knows it or not, if one does follow the laws of axiology in all one's valuation, choosing the axiological method serves one well, if only as a means for making one's valuations conscious—and hence to increase one's control over one's own life.

Once the axiom is accepted, the rest of axiology follows as a logical deduction from this axiom. The question of truth of the science of axiology does not enter into the matter at all because one will accept or reject the axiom depending on whether it is immediately evident or not, and immediate evidence is not truth in the common epistemological sense. Neither do the conclusions derived from this axiom leave room for the notion of truth, but only for the notion of validity. It is not a truth that two and two equals four but only a valid formula within the system of mathematics. Truth, in the epistemological sense, only enters into the matter when the system is applied, when, for example, one person says that there are two bottles of wine here and another says there are four. In this case, one of the two might be drunk and see four bottles while the other sees two. Only one proposition can be true: either there are two bottles or there are four, and the truth depends on whether there are two or four. None of this, however, concerns the validity of the arithmetic formula that two and two equals four. This validity follows exclusively—and conclusively— from the axiom which defines the number "one" and, following it, the rest of the numbers, and the operations between them; but it has nothing whatever to do with the truth of propositions which refer to things counted. In the same way, formal axiology is an axiomatic system which, as such, has nothing to do with value realities ex- cept that it can be applied to them. And such application can give rise to propositions that are true or false.

It is clear, then, that formal axiology as I shall present it is not a theory that can be either true or false, but a method of thinking that either functions or not, that is effective or ineffective in the sense described in the pre- ceding lecture. The verification of this science lies in the range of use that is made of it. I shall not say anything about this range of use at this point, but will leave you free to judge the axiom by itself without outside consid- erations. I shall, however, say something about this range in a later lecture.

Before discussing the matter of the axiom of formal axiology, we must first understand clearly what an axiom is. I remarked earlier that an axiom is the formal and symbolic formulation of the essence of a field of phenomena. Of prime importance here are the words "symbolic" and "formal," for they mean that we are now entering the field of language. We are not speaking of value phenomena, we are speaking of the language that accounts for them.

What, precisely, is a symbolic and formal formulation? There are formal symbols and non-formal symbols. The alphabet consists of symbols, a, b, c, etc., but it does not consist of formal symbols because, among the letters of the alphabet, there is no systematic connection: there is not a relationship among these letters, and it does not matter in what order they fall. There is somewhat more of a relationship among the words of everyday language, which are formed from these letters, but this connection is not inherent in the words themselves but lies only in the sense of these words which we learned as children. When I say that a man is a rational animal or that Theodore Roosevelt was president of the United States, we understand these statements because we understand the meaning of the words "man," "animal," "Theodore Roosevelt," "president," and "United States." It is not logically necessary that Theodore Roosevelt should have been president of the U.S.A., or that in 1980 Gerald Rumplemayer would be, as it is logically necessary that two and two equals four. If the former were logically necessary there would be no sense to politics or, for that matter, to life. In life, what rules is not so much necessity as contingency. Consequently, the statement, "Man is a rational animal," does not contain within itself a logical necessity but is a truth we have abstracted out of the concrete reality of our observation. The connection among these three words, "man," "animal," "rational," is contingent: it is implicit in our knowledge of life. These statements are either true or false but they are not valid or invalid as are the propositions "2+2=4" and "2+2=5." The connection among the symbols of these latter propositions is a logically necessary or faulty one within the system of mathematics.

The first distinctive characteristic of an axiom is that it gives rise to logically necessary propositions. The totality of such propositions is called a system. The second characteristic of an axiom is that such a system accounts for a vast field of real phenomena ("real" taken in the widest sense possible). This means that the system explains the phenomena: the totality of the phenomena in question must be organized and related in accordance with the system in question. If a system accounts for nothing it is mere fantasy, and such fantasies can be found in abundance in mental hospitals and even in daily life among crackpots and neurotics. Sometimes they can be found as hypotheses in science, but are quickly discarded when they are discovered to be ineffectual. An axiom, then, must combine the profound intellectual penetration of a phenomenon with the possibility of systematic development. It must combine practical import with theoretical import.

In a word, then, an axiom is that which has both practical and theoretical import. The theoretical import is the meaning or intension of the axiom, namely the system; and the practical import is its range of application or extension, namely the field of phenomena. The system makes these phenomena into the orderly world described earlier.

The axiom is the highest concept of science. There is also a highest concept of philosophy which is called category. Categories are concepts of highest generality such as "quantity," "quality," "relation," "purpose," "value," and so on. A category, too, has intension and extension. But its intension, or meaning does not consist of symbols interrelated by logical necessity but of predicates interrelated by contingency: by knowledge abstracted from concrete reality. The meaning of the category is implicit and not explicit as that of the axiom; and for this reason, as all implications in the sense described, is arbitrary. The dialectical logic of Hegel, for example, is made up of such categories, and their unravellings have the characteristics discussed in the last lecture, for they are not systematic but pseudo-systematic. All philosophy is the unfolding of some category and all science in the strict sense, is the unfolding of some axiom.

The difference between category and axiom, and thus the essence of the difference between philosophy and science, can be seen very clearly in the state of natural philosophy before and after Galileo. Both for Aristotle and for Galileo, the central concept of the theory of nature, of "physics," was the concept of movement or motion. For Aristotle, the definition of movement was "change from potentiality to actuality," "the movable qua movable," and the like. Aristotle developed these notions by more or less arbitrary and often fantastic implications. For Galileo, on the other hand, motion was represented as a simple, mathematical relation consisting of five symbols precisely interrelated: "$v = s/t$," "velocity equals space divided by time." This formula, of course, is today a basic relation of everyday life: if I travel one hundred miles in two hours, my speed is fifty miles an hour. This utterly simple and evident fact was so strange to Galileo's contemporaries that it produced a revolution. Galileo transformed Aristotelian movement, the metaphysical, ontological and theological cause of all happenings in the sublunar and supralunar world, into a seemingly trivial mathematical formula—a heresy which nearly cost him his life. He transformed a philosophic category into a scientific axiom.

What marvels occurred as a result of this little formula we all know. Galileo stated that once the axiom was found, no further observation was necessary, that all that was required was to derive conclusions from the formula. Having arrived at his formula by means of profound and ingenious experiments, he had no further need for observations but exclusively concentrated on the development of the formula, which would have to correspond to developments of phenomena in sense reality. The mere rudiments of algebra told him that if velocity is the division of space traveled by time elapsed, $v = s/t$, then s is equal to the product of v and t, $s = vt$, and from this immediately follows, by the mere rudiments of geometry, that s is equal to a rectangle with sides v and t which is equal to two triangles formed by the diagonals, that the angles between the sides and the diagonals are 45°, etc. etc. Without observing further velocities, balls that roll, or bodies that fall, Galileo proceeded to draw triangles and rectangles, learning, as he said, to speak the language of nature. In developing these geometrical figures and their formal relations he constructed, by means of pure geometry, the basis of the science of mechanics. This pattern was later developed by Newton, Newton's by Laplace, Laplace's by Einstein—and Einstein's was raped by politicians who today threaten us with atomic bombs. So potent, for good and evil, was the axiom contained in Galileo's little formula. From Aristotle's category of movement, none of this would have happened; we would not have the troubles that beset us, but neither would we have electric light and all the gadgets that make our lives so comfortable.

An axiom, therefore, is a powerful thing. It combines the maximum simplicity with the maximum efficacy.

We now come to the axiom of value. An axiom, as we have said, is the creation of an original thinker who sees, at a glance, the characteristic trait of a vast field of phenomena. Goethe thus saw the primary plant, the Urpflanze, while strolling under the palms of Palermo; Darwin, the pattern of evolution, on reading Malthus; Newton the law of gravitation, on feeling the impact of that famous apple. A generous literature exists about this type of experience—sometimes called the "Aha!" experience—in which occurs the ecstasy or shock of recognition. Sometimes, this shock has been physical, as in the case of Benjamin Franklin when he attracted lightning with his kite; sometimes it has occurred in a vision so overwhelming that the visionary has not been capable of completely realizing it, as in the case of Kepler.

This initial vision has already occurred in the realm of value. Its Benjamin Franklin, its Kepler, has already appeared. But, like many discoverers, he has not been understood. He saw value and maintained that it had an essence, that the entire realm had unity, and that examples could exhibit it but never exhaust it. He maintained that there is an essence of value which is not like anything else nor like any of its examples. To confuse it with anything else or with any of its examples, constitutes a fallacy. He further maintained that a science of value is not only possible but necessary and that it would bring about a new era in moral understanding.

The discoverer was George E. Moore. He came close to stating the structure of this essence and, for any careful reader, made utterly clear its axiomatic nature. Unfortunately, the philosophers of value did not understand him. Even supposing that he had captured value and brought it down from the skies, they were unable to follow up his experiment. Moore never told them how he built his kite or how he received his information. The experiment was not repeatable. And even though he outlined in detail the composition of the current, his words were so obscure as to be paradoxical, not only for his readers but for Moore himself. Thus, all he caused was a general admiring head-shaking. In spite of the fact that the axiom of the science of value was suggested in 1903, and stated—in a manner neither more nor less obscure than Kepler's laws of planetary motion—as early as 1922, the science of value is still unwritten. We must, today, rediscover G. E. Moore and write it.

We maintain, with Moore, that he wrote the Prolegomena to a science of value, and that what he said contains the essential truth about value: that it constitutes the axiom of scientific axiology. We will attempt to clarify this axiom, to develop it in a theoretical structure and show how this structure can be used to explain the phenomena of value.

Moore considered his book, *Principia Ethica*—whose title was modeled on the *Principia Mathematica Philosophiae Naturalis* of Newton, which was the basis for all future natural science—as the "Prolegomena to any future

Ethics that can possibly pretend to be scientific." In other words," he tells us, "I have tried to discover the fundamental principles of ethical reasoning." Scientific ethics deals not with the particular facts but with "all universal judgments which assert the relation of 'goodness' to any subject." It is "good in general." In form, Ethics is a science like physics or chemistry.

Moore, as we mentioned in the first lecture, after Plato and Kant, was the culminating thinker of the nonnaturalistic school of value. The thesis of his *Principia Ethica* is very simple: Good exists and it is not naturalistic but *sui generis*. What good is, unfortunately, Moore does not know. "Good is good and that is the end of the matter," is the key sentence in the book. Good is indefinable. And the motto of the book, taken from Bishop Butler is: "Everything is what it is and not another thing." Thus, the book is very short.

In spite of this it is the classic of a new age, for two reasons: its positive content and its negative content. Positively, the book very simply says that good is good and not something else. But his is an extremely important thesis because all philosophers between Plato and Moore, which represents the whole history of philosophy, have mixed good in itself with things that are good. They have said that good is pleasure, that good is satisfaction, that good is good will, that it is God, Being, evolution, and the like. But pleasure, satisfaction, good will, God, Being, evolution are things that are good, they are not good in itself. Pleasure is good, it makes us feel good, but pleasure is not the good. If pleasure were the good then to say pleasure is the good would be the same as saying that pleasure is pleasure. Moore called this identification of good with things that are good the naturalistic fallacy. Actually, it is a logical fallacy, that of defining a genus by a species rather than a species by a genus.

The negative content of the book consists in tracing this fallacy throughout the history of ethics and in demonstrating that all moral philosophy before Moore had been in error. Moore at least, and at last, opened the door to the correct question: What is good in itself? Although he did not answer the question, he made very clear that good in itself is that which all good things have in common. If I speak of a good button, of good Swiss cheese, of myself as a good person, or of God, the question is: What have all these goodnesses in common? What has the goodness of a button to do with the goodness of God, and what has the goodness of Swiss cheese to do with my own moral goodness? As far as Moore is concerned, goodness only knows!

Moore's first book appeared in 1903, and although he declared in it that good was indefinable, he spent the rest of his life determining it with increasing precision. Twenty years later he wrote and forty years later he clarified the basis for what we call, in these lectures, "formal axiology," namely, that "two different propositions are both true of goodness," (1) that good is not a natural property, and (2) that although this is so, good depends only on the natural properties of that which is called good. By "natural property" Moore means properties such as yellow or tall; any property that describes a thing, by which we may understand for simplicity's sake, any sensory property, that is, any property of a thing that we perceive through our senses—hearing, sight, taste, smell, touch—or through feeling in general. Although good is not a sensory property, it does depend entirely on the sensory properties of the thing that is called good. Let us see what this means.

If I say to someone, "I have a good automobile," what have I told him about my automobile? What does the person know about it? Many things. He knows that it has a motor that runs, an accelerator that accelerates, brakes that brake, tires, doors, seats, and so on. But he knows absolutely nothing that could identify, or describe the automobile. He knows nothing about the particular automobile in question. He does not know what make it is: Ford, Chevrolet or Oldsmobile; he does not know what type of automobile it is: convertible or sedan; if it has two or four doors; if it has white or black tires; if it has four, six, or eight cylinders. He knows nothing about my automobile; but "although this is so," he really knows many things about it. He knows all the properties which my automobile has in common with other automobiles, though he knows nothing about the specific properties of my particular automobile; and if I say to him: "I have a good automobile, go outside and look for it," he could never find it. Thus, good is not a natural property. Yet, it depends entirely on the natural properties of the thing which is called good. The goodness of my automobile depends entirely on its properties; for if my automobile brakes when I accelerate or accelerates when I brake, if it has no doors, no motor, no tires, then clearly it is not a good automobile.

This, then, is Moore's conclusion: good is not a natural property but nevertheless depends exclusively on the natural properties of that which is called good. If only one knew, he said, on what form it depended, one would know what good is. It is at this point that formal axiology enters and defines this "depend." The result is the axiom or fundamental definition of the scientific theory of value, to which Moore, in the work to which he devoted his life, has written the "Prolegomena."

Moore's conclusion was a riddle to him all his life. What does it mean to say that good is not a natural property and yet depends only on the natural properties of the thing that is good? The answer to the riddle is the following: Good is a property of concepts, not of objects. For a person to know that a thing "is good" it is not necessary for him to know anything about the particular thing in question, but he must know something about the concept of which this thing is an instance or example. In the case of an automobile, the person does not have to know anything about the specific automobile in question but he does have to know something about the concept "automobile," of which this particular automobile is an example. He must know what an automobile is, but he does not have to know how is my automobile. The word "good" does not refer to the knowledge of a particular automobile but to the knowledge of the concept "automobile." It qualifies the person's knowledge of this concept, that is, of the properties that all automobiles have in common. Whenever the word "good" is used, a logical operation occurs: the properties of the concept of a thing are combined with the image or idea of a particular thing which is said to be good. When we hear of a good automobile we combine the properties of the concept "automobile" which we have in our mind, with the image or idea of the particular automobile in question. We give this image all the properties we know automobiles possess, and thus form in our minds the image of a good automobile: an automobile that possesses all automobile properties. Upon the particular automobile, about which we may not know anything, we confer the properties of automobile in general, about which we should know something. And this is what we always do when we hear a thing spoken of as "good": we combine the properties of the concept of the thing with the idea of the thing in question. This logical operation is the meaning of the word "good." It tells us that we perform the following logical operation: Whenever a thing is called "a good C" then (1) the thing is meant to be a member of the class C and (2) it is meant to have all the properties which the intension of C indicates. This is expressed in the definition of good, as that which all good things have in common: A thing is good if, and only if, it fulfills the set of intensional properties of its concept.

This is the Axiom of Formal Axiology. It says, in the case of the good automobile, that (1) the thing called an "automobile" is an automobile, and (2) that it has all the automobile properties. The predicate of value, then, does not belong to individual things but to things as exemplifications of concepts. This solution of the logical nature of the value predicate corresponds exactly to the solution of the logical nature of arithmetical predicate, number, by Frege and subsequently Whitehead and Russell. The word "four" in "four white horses" is not a descriptive predicate like "white" but a predicate of a class "quartet," with which the white horses in question can be put into one-to-one correspondence. It is a formal or pattern word; only what it arranges are not extensions but intensions, it arranges sets of qualities, not of things. In the expression "good white horses" it arranges the qualities of whiteness and horsey-ness, or rather of white-horseyness. The horses in question are good white horses if they possess the total set of properties that the concept "white horse" connotes. "Good" signifies the totality of this set of properties.

This definition of good is a logical definition, because it defines value—the goodness of a thing—in terms of a logical relation, that of belonging to a class or class membership. It is also immediately evident, as you can convince yourselves by thinking or speaking a few sentences with "good." Whenever you want to say that a thing has the properties of some concept, say, "horse," you call it a good such thing, "a good horse."

From this simple definition of value now follow a multitude of consequences, all corollaries of the axiom, and vital for the concept of value and its age-old problems. I shall mention the following seven:

1. The Difference between Value in General and Value in Particular

It is clear that the value defined is value in general and neither ethical nor aesthetic, nor metaphysical, nor economic, nor any specific kind of value. It is simply Value, that is, formal or axiological value. In this way we have avoided the moral fallacy of defining value in general in terms of specific values, and the metaphysical fallacy of explaining value in terms of nature. We have created our own autonomous axiom for the science of value.

2. Absolute Value

The age-old inquiry concerning the absolute norm of value is: What is the universal norm or standard in comparison with which every value is determined? The answer is very simple: the norm of value for each thing is its name. Norm equals name. At one blow, this resolves the hundreds of problems that have arisen around absolute value, the standard of value, posed and answered metaphysically, that is, evaded throughout the centuries. In the same way, many problems in natural science, such as that of the number $\sqrt{-1}$, of the irrational number and others, were discussed metaphysically before the mathematical frame of reference for them was found.

The rule that the norm of each thing is its name, that is, the name's meaning or intension, is also applicable to value itself: the norm of value is the meaning or intension of the name "value." This meaning or intension has just been given by the axiom of value: it is "the fulfillment of an intension." Insofar as something is the fulfillment of an intension, it is value. The axiom of value thus states the norm of all value. It is absolute value.

3. Axiological Positivism

The logical definition of value which serves as the axiom for the axiological system, signifies a nominalism or axiological positivism. Positivism commits four out of the five axiological fallacies: the metaphysical fallacy by confusing the natural frame of reference with the axiological; the fallacy of method by concluding from the inapplicability of the natural frame to value (that is, from the lack of an axiological frame of reference) to the irrationality of value itself; the empirical fallacy by confusing natural or empirical science with science in general; and the naturalistic fallacy by reducing ethics to sociology, psychology, anthropology, and the like. Formal axiology, by providing an axiological frame of reference for value phenomena alongside the mathematico-logical frame of reference for natural phenomena, establishes axiological positivism alongside logical positivism.

4. The Rationality of Valuation

At the root of our procedure is the implicit presupposition—which is not an explicit part of the axiological system but is confirmed by the effect and the effectiveness of the system—that the world of value can be rationally explained. This does not mean that the world is rational—to assert this would be to commit the fallacy of method—but it does mean that it is rational to the extent that it can be ordered by the axiological system, for to order the world is part of the world.

From the fact that the definition of value is rational, it follows that valuation is rational and that the more I know about a thing the better I can value it. This also corresponds to the facts; for we call in an expert when we want to evaluate something with accuracy. The difference between us and the expert is that the expert is better acquainted with the properties of the thing to be valued than we. Valuational precision is not quantitative but qualitative. It is not a precision of measure but of meaning. The expert determines the properties of a thing with precision and compares them with those contained in the meaning of the thing's concept. This concept, the normal concept of the thing, thus becomes the normative concept for the thing.

5. The Objectivity of Value

Axiological value is objective: every rational being uses it. It is valid for any human being, man, woman or child, of whatever culture or nationality and even for any rational being whatever, whether on this earth or some other star in the universe: If one thinks rationally, that is, if concepts are logically joined and related to objects, then there is a word which means that the thing referred to has all the properties of its concept. This word, in our language, is "good," "Bueno," "gut," "dobrze," etc. It is a logical word, a predicate of a set of predicates: it says that a thing is in possession of all its descriptive predicates. In being a predicate of predicates it is a second-order predicate. "Goodness" has a logical meaning as exact as any mathematical term, and as objective as "2 x 2 = 4."

While formal axiology is objective, its application, as the application of any science, is subjective. If our above-mentioned drunk says that he sees four bottles where I see only two, he does not invalidate arithmetic but only applies it incorrectly. If I say that a thing is good and you say that it is bad, we do not invalidate axiology, we only apply it differently; in reality, we confirm it by our difference. I say that a thing is good because, applying axiology, I believe that it has all the properties of its concept; and you call it bad, also applying axiology, in the belief that it does not have all the properties of its concept (which is the axiological definition of "bad"). Consequently, it can easily be seen that there are many reasons for axiological discord just as there are many reasons for mathematical error: a thing can be seen wrongly, it can be thought that a thing has a name other than the one it has—perceptual reasons and conceptual reasons—but in every case axiology is applied and the disagreement is defined in accordance with it.

6. Optimism and Pessimism

The mere axiom also explains the difference between the valuational temperaments, such as the optimistic and pessimistic. Since a thing is good when it has all the properties of its concept and bad when it does not have them all, and since, on the other hand, any set of properties can be fulfilled by some concept, it is possible that one and the same set of properties may be fulfilled by one concept and hence be good with respect to it, but not be fulfilled by another concept, and hence be bad with respect to it. As Spinoza had already observed, a good ruin is a bad house, and a bad house is a good ruin. The talent of the optimist consists in always seeing the concept that fulfills a set of properties, and the pessimist's talent consists in seeing the concept that does not fulfill it. While the pessimist says that he has a bad car, the optimist declares that he has a "beautiful jalopy"; the pessimist hears a bad song, the optimist a good try; for the pessimist, the glass of water is half empty, for the optimist it is half full. Instead of a glass of water, it can be said that for the pessimist any concept will be half "empty" and for the optimist it will be half "full." The optimist, therefore, sees more of the concrete and abstract world than the pessimist.

Since for the optimist the appropriate concept is always compatible with the intension or meaning in question, and for the pessimist the non-appropriate concept seems always compatible, it can be generally said that good is the compatibility and bad the incompatibility between concepts and intensions. As any intension seemingly compatible with an inappropriate concept is actually compatible with its appropriate concept, bad is the transposition of appropriate with inappropriate concepts. Since correct thinking means the compatibility between a thing and the concept appropriate to it, the pessimist does not think correctly. He is, as the philosopher Peirce has said, "a little insane." The true realist is the optimist. Much of the evil in the world has come from its being run by pessimists. It takes optimists to set the world aright (that is why Hamlet's was a hopeless case).

7. The Goodness of the World

From the axiom also issues the answer to the age-old question of whether the world is good or bad. The concept proper to the world is "the world" and its intension contains all the properties that there are, were, or have been in the world; it is the totality of all possible properties. The world in its totality fulfills this intension and is therefore good, even though no actual world does. Furthermore, it must be observed that this goodness is neither ethical nor metaphysical, but axiological. The world, as the world, can be neither more nor less than a good world. But the things in the world are both good and bad. The world contains the maximum axiological variety in unity.

Of course, all this sounds extremely simple. Perhaps, you will think, it is so simple as to really mean nothing at all. But I would like to remind you of the nature of the axiom: it combines the greatest simplicity with the greatest efficacy. Today we have demonstrated its simplicity, tomorrow we shall demonstrate its efficacy.

Lecture IV

THE DIMENSIONS
OF VALUE AND THE
SCIENCE OF VALUE

ABSTRACT

In this Lecture, Hartman expands upon the axiom of value that he introduced in the preceding lecture. Here, he elaborates upon that axiom by describing the three types of concepts and the type of value that applies to each type of concept. He provides a logical justification for this tripartite hierarchy of value by way of transfinite mathematics. He then describes in detail the three types of value: systemic, extrinsic, and intrinsic, and concludes by outlining an axiological taxonomy of various academic disciplines such as ethics, psychology, sociology, and political science.

In the previous lecture, which dealt with the axiom of value, an axiom was defined as the combination of maximum simplicity with maximum efficiency. The simplicity of the axiom has already been discussed and it now remains for us to examine its efficiency.

It will be remembered that Galileo's little formula for motion made the difference between Aristotle's category of movement and Galileo's axiomatic of motion. It represents the difference between the old, speculative natural philosophy and the precise modern natural science. In much the same way our little formula for value, which states that the value of a thing depends on the degree to which the thing fulfills its concept, makes the difference between the category of value and an axiomatic of value; it represents the difference between the old speculative moral philosophy and a precise future moral science.

In philosophy, the category of value consists of words such as Pleasure, Will of God, Purpose, and so on. While these words contain implications, they contain no explications, in the sense of explicit directions for the development of a system. The axiom of value, on the other hand, does explicitly give such directions, and by the mere fact of its symbolic configuration. This configuration is as simple as was the simple relation of division by which Galileo defined velocity.

What, then, is the formula of value? The axiom of value says that a thing is good in the degree to which it fulfills its concept and is not good in the degree to which it does not fulfill it. The concept of a thing contains the names of certain numbers of properties; for example, the concept "chair" contains the names of four properties, that is, predicates, which define this concept: "a knee-high structure with a seat and a back." The four properties are: structure, knee-high, seat, and back. A chair that has all of these properties is a good chair, and a chair that lacks some of these properties, such as a seat or a back, or has no structure but wobbles, is not a good chair although it might be a good stool or a good device for acrobats. Of course, a chair has many more than these four properties, since each of these properties has its own properties, and the properties of the properties also have properties, and so on. As a result, a chair, as any other thing, contains an enormous number of conceptual properties; and the degree to which it fulfills or does not fulfill this collection of properties can vary widely—yet, can be calculated with precision. It is this characteristic which gives valuation its interesting quality.

We can say, then, that the concept of a thing contains a certain number of predicates or property names or, for short though logically not quite correct, of properties. Let us call the number of these properties n. Whenever a thing referred to by the name of a concept, say the name "chair," contains the n properties of this concept, it is a good such thing. If it contains less than n properties of the concept, it is not a good such thing. From this little formula are derived the other valuational terms such as, "fair," "average," "bad," etc. Very simply, we can define a thing as fair if it contains more properties of the concept than it lacks and as bad if it lacks more properties of the concept than it has. In other words, it is fair if it has more than half of the properties of its concept, and bad if it has less than half of those properties. If it is neither good nor bad, it will then contain exactly half of the properties of its concept, which we define as average value.

It can now be seen how simple the understanding of valuation becomes. The value good is represented by n; the value average is represented by one half of n; the value fair is represented by more than one half of n; and the value bad by less than one half of n. The possible values of a thing such as a chair, then, are n, half of n, half of n plus a number that is less than this half, let us say m, and half of n less the number m. There are, in other words, n, n/2, n/2+m, and n/2-m. Now something curious happens.

The sum of the possible values of a thing is the sum of the values stated, that is, n+(n/2)+(n/2+m)+(n/2-m). As can be readily seen, the total is 2 1/2n. Thus, if a thing has 10 properties, the sum of all its possible values—its goodness plus its average plus its fairness plus its badness is 25. Naturally, this appears to be quite strange. How can a thing that only has 10 properties, have 25 values? How are these ten converted into 25?

For anyone who knows the mathematics of combination and permutation, the answer is obvious. Any number n of elements can be arranged in a certain number of sub-elements. For example, if you have two elements, these can be arranged in three different ways: the first 1, the second 1, and the two together. The general formula for the number of possible subsets of a set of elements n is 2n-1. If n equals 2, then we have 2 to the power of 2 which equals 4, minus 1 which equals three. If we have three elements, the corresponding number is 7; if we have four elements the number is 15; and if we have ten elements, as in the above example, the corresponding number of possible sub-groups is 1023. Each sub-set is a value. Each value then is a set of properties. Conversely, each set of properties is a value. Thus, we may define value, and state our axiom, in arithmetical rather than logical language: The total value of a thing is the totality of the sub-sets of the thing's set of descriptive properties. A thing of 1023 properties has 1023 different values whose totality is the thing's total value. It is not surprising, then, that 25 properties can result from 10. Actually the sum of the values contained in a thing is not very large. The product is much greater and shows, moreover, a great but exactly definable variety. In the case of 10 properties one kind of value product consists of 453,600,000,000 properties.

What does this tell us about valuation? It tells us that valuation is nothing more nor less than a dispensing with things and an operation with pure properties. In a way, valuation is a playing with properties, as music is a playing with sounds. The properties of things, abstracted from the things, could be called the sounds of valuation. Formal axiology is the musical score for those pure properties: it gives us the combinations and the keys. The set of properties itself is the thing as fact; the combinations of the properties are the values of the thing; and the keys are the dimensions of value.

So far, we have been interpreting the axiom of value numerically. We shall now interpret it metrically, and by employing the notion of measurement, open up the field of value in its whole expanse.

Let us remember again, the axiom of value: a thing has value in the degree to which it fulfills its concept, and it lacks value, or has dis-value, in the degree to which it does not fulfill its concept. The concept, then is the measure of value. We employ it to measure the value of a thing or, conversely, we measure the value of thing by its concept. For example, we measure the value of a chair by the concept "chair." If a chair has all the properties in the concept chair, then it is a good chair; and in the degree to which it lacks some of the properties of this concept, it is a bad chair. The concept serves as the measure of the value of a thing, just as a yardstick serves as the measure of the length of a thing. As the inches are contained in the yard, so the predicates are contained in the concept. The concept is to value what the yardstick is to length. And as we use different measurement apparatus for different things—a tape to measure the circumference of a tree, for instance, since it would be impossible to do so with a yardstick (except by multiplying with π)—so we use different conceptual measurements for different things. We measure the value of chairs by the concept "chair," of pears by the concept "pear," or of professors by the concept "professor." But all these measures are concepts. Since all of us carry the concepts of things in our minds, we carry in our minds, also, the yardsticks or tapes of the value of things. When we call a thing good we are saying that it has a plenitude of the measures of its value, which we have in our minds; and when we call a thing bad we are saying that it does not have a plentitude of this measure.

As we stated earlier, there are two kinds of concepts: axiomatic or formal concepts, and abstract concepts. The former are constructed, the latter are abstracted. Axiomatic concepts, such as the concepts of science—"number, "circle," "electron"—are constructed in the mind. Abstract concepts are abstracted by the mind from things belonging to the concrete world, such as the concept "chair." Remember, there is, in addition a third class of

concepts called singular concepts which are neither constructed nor abstracted, but which contain the totality
of properties of an individual thing, such as the concept
"this chair," or the concept "Franklin D. Roosevelt," or
the concept "my uncle John."

There are very significant differences in the structure
of these concepts and there are, consequently, very significant differences in their fulfillments. Since the value
of a thing is the fulfillment of its concept there arise from
the different conceptual structures different structures or
dimensions, of value: systemic value, extrinsic value, and
intrinsic value.

Let us first discuss the distinctive characteristics of
the three kinds of concepts. The axiomatic or formal
concept forms part of a system. The concept "four" or
the number 4, the concepts "square root of minus one,"
or the number "i," are concepts within the system of
mathematics. Within this system they are defined with
precision. They either have the properties of their definition or they do not. There are no bad numbers 4 nor bad
square roots of minus one. The same is true of all scientific concepts such as the geometrical concept "circle,"
or the physical concept "electron." A bad circle is simply
not a circle but an ellipse or some other figure, and a bad
electron is not an electron but another particle. All of
the recent developments in physics might be said to be
the classifications of "bad" electrons, which are not electrons. The reason for this limitation is that these things

are defined with such precision (and the word "definition" means limitation) that the smallest deviation from the definition means that a thing is not what it is called. Systemic things, then, have only two values: perfection and non-existence. The distinctive characteristic of the systemic or formal concept is that it has a minimum number of predicates.

The abstract concept, too, has a significant characteristic. We can abstract only if we have at least two things, for abstraction means that we pull off, so to speak—this is the literal meaning of the Latin *abs-trahere*—the properties that things have in common; and, naturally, properties cannot be in common, unless there are at least two things. The number 2, then, is the lower extensional limit of abstraction. But there is no upper limit to the number of things from which common properties can be abstracted. Only that, the greater the number of things, the smaller the number of properties they will have in common and hence can be abstracted. If we take all the things that are, they will have only one property in common, that of being—they all are: and this is not saying much.

Since the philosophical discipline of ontology has being as its object, it is easy to understand why the philosopher as an ontologist has to go through the contortions and word plays which we observe, for example, in Heidegger. On the other hand, the more "precise" he becomes in his use of words, as for example Spinoza or Paul Weiss, the more problems arise, due to the unlimited contents and implications, of even the most "precisely" defined concepts. But if one has only two things, which is the lower limit of abstraction, a great deal can be said about what properties they have in common. It is a rule of fundamental logic that the higher abstracted is a concept the less meaning it has, and the less abstracted it is the more meaning it has. This fundamental rule cannot be invalidated by the subtleties philosophers have employed to show up exceptions to the rule. These are in every case exceptions which confirm the rule (as Ernst Cassirer has shown in his work *Substance and Function*). And this rule can certainly not be invalidated by a logic, such as that of the positivists, which dispenses with meaning altogether. Actually, two things can have an infinity of properties in common. The number of properties contained in an abstract concept, therefore, is between one and infinity. This is the first distinctive characteristic of abstraction. The second is that each of the common properties must be abstracted by itself, one by one, because I must search my mind and find each property that the things in question have in common. This means that the set or collection of these properties must be discrete or discontinuous; each common property must be taken by itself. The characteristic of abstraction, then, is that predicates within an abstract concept are a set of infinite discontinuous elements.

The singular concept, in which is contained the totality of properties of an individual thing, also has a distinctive feature. When I look at this chair or think of Franklin

Delano Roosevelt or my uncle John, I am neither abstracting nor constructing. Rather, I am imagining or depicting. I have in my mind an image, or, using the psychological term, a Gestalt, of the form of this very chair, of the unique and singular Franklin Delano Roosevelt or my uncle John. In the case of my uncle John, he has a thick nose with a wart which turns blue in the winter and which in the summer has a small hole on its left side. This hole has a little crease which is black, which blackness varies in color according to his emotional state, and so on and so on. Naturally, there is a great deal more to my uncle John than the blackness of the crease of the hole of the wart on his nose. In fact, the properties of a singular concept are infinite; but they are infinite in a manner different from those of the abstract concept. They are not discontinuous, they do not exist by themselves; isolated; rather, they are continuous one with the other. The distinctive characteristic of the singular concept is that the predicates within it are a set of infinite, continuous elements; they form a continuum.

In summary, the distinctive feature of the formal concept is that its intension has a minimum number of properties; the distinctive feature of the abstract concept is that its intension has a group of, potentially or actually, infinite discontinuous properties; and the distinctive feature of the singular concept is that its intension has an infinite set of continuous properties.

Up to this point we have characterized the three classes of concepts by common sense, or if you will, phenomenologically. The next step is to do what the creative scientist does and find a formal pattern which systematically accounts for all that has been said. Furthermore, if this system is to be a genuine system, it will not only account for all the foregoing but a great deal more. When Galileo discovered the arithmetical relation of division between time and distance and defined it as velocity, he found more than he was looking for: he placed the phenomenon of motion within the system of mathematics which latter, of course, contains much more than the simple relation of division. By extending Galileo's simple equations, Newton discovered the laws of gravity and Einstein the theory of relativity. When a scientist discovers a system he always finds more than he is looking for. This characteristic of science is called serendipity, from Walpole's story *The Princes of Serendip* (Ceylon), who, being on the right track, always found more than they were looking for.

What is needed, then, is a system which will contain the distinctive characteristics of the three classes of concepts: 1) definite sets of elements; 2) infinite sets of discontinuous elements; 3) infinite sets of continuous elements.

Such a system happens already to exist, fully elaborated, in the field of mathematics: the mathematics of the so-called transfinite numbers. In this system, the finite collection of elements is called n, that is, any integer; the infinite collection of discontinuous elements is called aleph zero, the first letter of the

Hebrew alphabet; and the infinite collection of continuous elements, or the continuum, is called aleph one (we shall denote "aleph" by   " $\aleph$ "). Using the precisely defined operations among three classes of numbers, we obtain a beautifully clear calculus of valuation.

In other words, the mathematical system of transfinite numbers is isomorphic with the realm of values and symbolically formulates the vast field of valuation, reflecting in systematic detail all that philosophers have said about value and, more significantly, what they have not said.

The details of this calculus are too complex for this survey. An electronic firm in Texas used an IBM 650 electronic computer to prepare a table of value and valuational situations, much like a logarithmic table. This table has some 300 pages and 30,000 value formulae. As an example, the formula for the situation of the pilot of the Enola Gay who, after dropping the bomb on Hiroshima, wrote in his log: "My God, what have we done?" is as follows: $(I_S)_I$, meaning the intrinsic devaluation of the systemic devaluation of an intrinsic value; the terror of the pilot $(\ )_I$ on seeing the military disintegration $(\ _S)$ of men, women and children $(I\ )$.

We can get an idea of the three dimensions of value with which this calculus operates: systemic, extrinsic, and intrinsic value.

These dimensions of value are based, as we have seen, on the three classes of concepts. The value of a thing is the degree to which it fulfills its concept. The fulfillment of a formal concept is systemic value, the fulfillment of an abstract concept is extrinsic value, and the fulfillment of a singular concept is intrinsic value.

Systemic value is the value of conformity to a system. It applies to anything that is part of a system, such as the square root of minus one, or the geometrical circle. Since the formal concept contains a minimum of properties, systemic valuation can be based on very few properties. Also, since this kind of valuation only knows two values, perfection or non-existence, it sees everything as dichotomy, as either white or black. There are people who regard Blacks as bad because they are black, and Whites as good because they are white. This is a misapplication of systemic value, regarding humans as elements in the system of spectroscopy. Prejudice is misapplied systemic value. Political systems which require conformity of the individual are based on systemic valuations. This valuation fits square roots and exponents, but not people. It is correct for mental constructions but not for humans. The confusion of humans, including oneself, with a mental construction is a well-known psychological phenomenon (a neurosis) which becomes elucidated by the axiology of systemic value. On the other hand, the empirical findings of psychology in this respect confirm in every point the formal deductions of axiology in the field of systemic value.

Extrinsic value is the value of comparison; it values things within, and as members of, classes. A good chair is a better chair than a bad chair but it cannot be said that a good chair is better than a good horse. The chair has chair-goodness and the horse has horse-goodness, and since chair and horse do not belong to the same class they cannot be compared. They are not subject to being measured by the same axiological yardstick, chairs being measured by the concept chair, and horses by the concept horse. We could measure chair and horse extrinsically, that is compare them, only if we could find a class common to both. There is a class common to all concrete things like chairs and horses. The concept of this class is the concept of price and its range or extension is the totality of all economic articles, from a pin to a battleship. Here appears the science of economics as an application of axiology (and by an argument which is identical with Aristotle's foundation of this science, *(Nic. Ethics 1133b).* Economics is defined as the application of extrinsic value to things. That economic value is the only extrinsic value common to all the concrete things that are, means axiologically something precise and detailed, and gives structure to the old and not yet resolved arguments on the foundations of money. It also explains the importance of economics in our lives, which is not accident. But it is only one of the values and not, as some think, value itself.

If not the totality of all extrinsic things is under consideration, but only specific sections of things, particularly if the things under consideration are conceptually close, then things can be compared in aspects other than the economic. Apples and mangoes can be compared under the concept fruit. Although we cannot say that a good mango is better than a good apple, we can say that a good mango is a better fruit than a good apple, and vice versa. Men can be compared extrinsically when they are members of classes, such as trolley car conductors, bakers, doctors, secretaries and the like. We cannot say that a good baker is better than a good trolley car conductor but we can say that a good baker is better than a bad baker. The science which deals with people compared in classes is Sociology, which here appears as an application of axiology. It is defined as extrinsic value applied to a group of persons.

Intrinsic value is the value of the thing in itself, based on the fulfillment of a singular concept. The concept is neither abstracted nor constructed. How then is it possible to value an individual thing in the totality of its infinite properties? Obviously when we talk of this chair, or of Franklin Delano Roosevelt, or of my uncle John, we do not think of them in the totality of their properties but only in the degree, not necessarily large, to which we know them. On the other hand, if I talk of my wife, or you talk of your husband or your son, we are talking about people we know intimately through familiarity, not by abstraction or construction. Indeed, complete knowledge of a singular thing is the complete identification with the thing in question. The painter who paints a chair identifies himself with the chair, reproducing all of its characteristics in the infinity of its aspects and, as artists have expressed it, actually becoming the chair. One has only to think of Van Gogh's famous painting *Portrait of a Chair.* The chair has personality; its personality is that of the artist himself. The branch of knowledge which deals with such identifications with things in art, is called Aesthetics, which we here see growing naturally out of axiology. It is defined as intrinsic value applied to things.

We can now observe how axiology relates fields of phenomena that were previously without any mutual relation, as Aesthetics and Economics. Economics being the application of extrinsic value to things, the difference between Economics and Aesthetics is simply the difference between extrinsic and intrinsic valuation applied to things. Since this relation is precisely defined in the system of axiology, as the relation between aleph one and aleph zero, the difference between Aesthetics and Economics is defined with equal precision. In this precise relation between aleph one and aleph zero, it is immediately evident that aesthetic is an infinitely more valuable value—in the sense of the words infinitely more as defined by the relation between aleph one and aleph zero—than economic value. It is, therefore, infinitely more valuable to consider a thing aesthetically than economically; and, therefore, my aesthetic pleasure on viewing my Orozco is of infinitely greater value than any sum of money that might be offered me for it. It is also evident that the business of buying and selling paintings has nothing whatever to do with aesthetics. Hence the many phony values of this trade.

There are all degrees of viewing an individual thing, from superficial acquaintance with it to most intimate familiarity, to the point of identification. These degrees of intrinsic valuation, which have nothing to do with either abstraction or construction, are called degrees of differentiation. Differentiation is to the singular thing what exemplification is to the particular thing, the thing belonging to a class. Differentiation might be called singular exemplification and its contrary, the lack of differentiation, may be called singular abstraction, as is done by Susanne Langer. Or, exemplification might be called the differentiation of a particular thing, a thing within a class, as is done by Plato and Aristotle in the famous *diaresis* or division. A singular thing is known in qualitative degree, that is, the degree to which the majority of its characteristics are known intimately, or, in other words, in the degree to which the thing is differentiated in detail. Intrinsic abstraction, then, is within the intrinsic key or dimension of a thing the opposite of intrinsic differentiation. The less differentiated a thing is, the more it is singularly abstracted and the more differentiated it is, the less it is singularly abstracted. The upper limit of differentiation is seeing the thing as oneself and hence fully as itself (Husserl's *Selbstgebung*); it is identification with the thing. The lower limit is seeing the thing as numerically one. The former is to see the thing in singular intension of meaning, the latter is to see it in singular extension. The former is the perception of the thing as unique, the latter is the perception of the thing as one.

The most important singular thing that each one of us possesses is himself. Each of us is given to himself and our task in life consists in knowing ourselves more and more, in familiarizing ourselves with ourselves more deeply, in becoming increasingly more who we are. Psychologically, this means becoming more and more integrated; axiologically, it means becoming more and more differentiated. The completely differentiated person is one who completely fulfills his concept of himself, which is the concept "I". According to our definition of value, such a person is a good person, and this goodness is the one we define as moral goodness. The various expressions for moral goodness, such as sincere, genuine, honest, authentic, true to himself, all mean being completely who one is. This moral goodness is the subject matter of Ethics which is defined as intrinsic valuation applied to the individual person, or the "I". Here we see how Ethics grows naturally out of axiology.

Again, observe how axiology connects what was formerly unconnected, such as Ethics and Sociology, Ethics and Aesthetics, Ethics and Economics, to name a few. The differences between Sociology and Ethics is the difference between extrinsic valuation applied to groups and intrinsic valuation applied to individual persons. For this reason it is infinitely more valuable to be a morally good person, in the strictly defined meaning of infinity, than to be a good trolley car conductor, baker, or professor. I am moral in the degree that I am who I am, not in the degree that I do what I am doing.

It is also evident how axiology can discover or define new sciences. If Sociology is extrinsic value applied to groups of persons and Ethics is intrinsic valuation applied to individual persons, then there must be a science that is extrinsic valuation applied to individual persons and another that is intrinsic valuation applied to groups of persons. The first, extrinsic valuation applied to individual persons, deals with individual persons as a class of functions and is Psychology; the second, intrinsic valuation applied to groups of persons, deals with groups of persons, identified with a common cause, and is Political Science.

The difference between moral and sociological or social value has been fascinatingly dealt with in works of literature, such as Tolstoy's short novel *The Death of Ivan Ilych*. Ivan Ilych is a judge in a provincial Russian court and has all the dignity and pomposity of his profession. His appointment as a judge of the Supreme Court fulfills a lifetime ambition and one day, while arranging the curtains in his new house in Moscow, he falls from the ladder, breaking a rib and doing fatal damage to his liver. His consciousness of imminent death awakens in him a consciousness of the futility and worthlessness of all his former values and he becomes aware of the importance of the "I" of him, or himself as this human being, and of other human beings. As time goes by neither his colleagues nor his own family concern themselves with him, and his only friend turns out to be his dull-witted servant who relieves his pain and makes him comfortable. The story is a poignant description of the infinite superiority of the moral over the social values. A more recent literary effort on the same subject is Boris Pasternak's *Dr. Zhivago* which explains why its publication was banned in Russia. A government based entirely on social value would fail if moral values would become supreme.

The relation between Ethics and Aesthetics lies in intrinsic valuation as applied to persons and intrinsic valuation applied to things. It can be demonstrated that a person is of infinitely greater value than a thing, for it is the only thing which contains within itself its own definition. He is the thinking thing, as Descartes said. This relation to himself is of an infinite nature, as the German mathematician Dedekind demonstrated a hundred years before axiology was conceived. Although a thing, considered intrinsically, has an infinity of properties, a person, considered intrinsically, has a greater infinity of properties. His value is not aleph one but aleph two or even higher. The subject matter of Ethics, therefore, is of an infinitely higher value than the subject matter of Aesthetics; and to consider life ethically is of an infinitely higher value than to consider it aesthetically. This is the message of Kierkegaard's classic on the relation between Ethics and Aesthetics, *Either/Or*, written more than one hundred years before axiology. Kierkegaard's ethics is exactly the ethics that also results from the system of axiology. The relation between Ethics and Sociology, or between ethical and social value, is minutely described by Kierkegaard in his *Point of View*, and in parts of his classic *The Sickness Unto Death*.

The difference between Ethics and Economics is the difference between the application of intrinsic value to persons and the application of extrinsic value to things. Since intrinsic value is infinitely more valuable than extrinsic value, aleph one being infinitely more infinite in the mathematical sense, than aleph zero, and since persons are infinitely more valuable than things, the ethical aspect is infinitely more valuable than the economic aspect. It is, therefore, profoundly evil to confuse the moral and economic values, as for example, to sell one's child to an old lecher (as was done by the parents of 12 year old Rita Flynn, in Joliet, Ill., who sold her, for $28,000, to Harold Miller of Oak Park, Ill.), to sell a person into slavery, or to degrade a moral value such as love, by selling it in prostitution. Intellectually, it is profoundly evil to subordinate a moral value to an economic value, and when this occurs within a political system it is, as measured by axiological science, an evil system in the strict definition of this term. For this reason, when I was young, I was certain of the fall of Nazism in spite of its triumphs in war and in the world in general. I have also experienced the absence of moral value in Communism and am sure it will either reform or break it. In 1953, when I lectured in a number of German Universities, among the students were some from the Communist University of East Berlin who told me that although they were convinced communists, they were profoundly disturbed by the lack of an articulated human—as against collective—morality within the Communist system. Historically, we know that revolutions within a system arise from the conflict between the systemic values of the system and the intrinsic values of the human person. However, this conflict is not limited to totalitarian systems, but only pronounced in them to the point of producing intolerable tensions. Any government is a system dominated, to a large extent, by systemic values. The art of governing consists in adjusting as much as possible the systemic values—of bureaucracy, red tape and so on—to human values. Gian-Carlo Menotti's opera *The Consul* is a dramatic presentation of the interrelation between the systemic values of both a totalitarian and democratic system, on the one hand, and the intrinsic value of a human being, on the other. The democratic system in question is that of the United States. We have all experienced the systemic arrogance, the moral indifference, and the fall of the highest Nixon appointees.

Let us now summarize the three dimensions of value in an example.

The best example for illustrating the interrelation of the three dimensions of value is love. Love is, of course, the value phenomenon par excellence. Let us take, as an example, a young mathematics student, John, who is going to Europe for his summer vacation. As he boards the Queen Mary, he says to himself, "I'm going to have myself a time!" In his mind is the image of a curve, undulating in character which belongs to the concept girl. At this moment, this is nothing but a systemic concept, for he is thinking of no girl in particular but only of what might be called the principle of femininity. The second day out there is a dance and, as is customary on European ships, the girls are lined up on one side of the hall and the young men on the other. As he stares at the young ladies opposite, his valuation changes from systemic to extrinsic, for he is seeing real girls, examples of the class girl, from whom the common properties of the abstract concept girl had been abstracted. His extrinsic valuation consists in applying the yardstick of this concept girl to the example of girlhood before him, to see which one of them fulfills this concept to the greatest degree, that is, which one has the greatest number of the properties of girl, weighing, as it were—and it is interesting to note that the Greek word *axios* is the English axle, meaning the axle of a scale—weighting, as it were, the girls against their own girl-measure, namely girl.

He finally decides on one of the girls and dances with her. While they dance, the same process of extrinsic valuation continues; he compares what he has in his arms with what he has in his mind. He dances with a few other girls and finally decides that one of them, Betty, is the best girl, which does not mean that she is morally the best but rather that, to the greatest degree, she fulfills the properties in question. He has a glorious voyage. But the day before the ship is due to arrive at Southampton, something happens to him that seems utterly irrational and can only be explained by formal axiology. When he awakens in the morning, a thought suddenly takes hold of him: Betty is not just a girl, a member of the class of girls who can be compared to other girls, but believe it or not, she is the only girl in the world and incomparable! He knows full well that there are one thousand million girls in the world, yet, he knows with equal certainty, and actually with greater certainty, that Betty is the only girl in the world. From this he logically concludes that since he is a man and a man cannot live without a woman, and since she is the only woman in the world, he must live with her. He writes her an extremely strange letter, filled with poetic words and such metaphors as "my treasure," "my world," "light of my life," and also axiological words like "my only one," "incomparable one," telling her that she must marry him and, adding in a postscript that if she doesn't he will throw himself overboard. All this from a mathematician.

Of course, we all know what has happened to John. Axiologically, it is the transition from systemic valuation to extrinsic and from extrinsic to intrinsic valuation up to complete identification. John and Betty marry and live happily ever after—up to a point. For after several months or years of married life, the process suddenly reverses itself. While John is walking along the street one day he notices that there are other girls in the world, and begins to compare Betty with them, and a little while later he even goes back to systemic valuation, valuing her as his housekeeper, an element in the routine of his home, and he becomes angry when the soup is not ready on time or when she squeezes the toothpaste tube at the top while he squeezes it at the bottom. He scolds her for being so disorganized—and when she begins to cry, his heart melts and she becomes again the one and only woman in the world. So in our lives we constantly swing from one dimension of value to another. Formal axiology is the norm that clarifies these situations for us.

The following is the synoptic table of the axiological sciences.

APPLICATION TO	INTRINSIC VALUE	EXTRINSIC VALUE	STSTEMIC VALUE
Individual Persons	Ethics	Psychology	Physiology Jurisprudence of "Person"
Groups of Persons	Political Science Social Ethics	Sociology	Law of Persons and Institutions
Individual Things	Aesthetics	Economics	Technology
Groups of Things	Science of Civilization	Ecology	Industrial Technology Civil Engineering Games Law of Property Ritual
Concepts	Metaphysics	Epistemology	Logic
Words	Poetry Literary Criticism	Rhetoric Semantic Linguistic Analysis	Grammar Theory of Communication

The detailed elaboration of all these sciences cannot be the task of either one or a dozen men, but a task for generations to come. For the time being, we have serious beginnings of the following value sciences: ethics, psychology, psychiatry, aesthetics, economics, and metaphysics. In psychology, especially, we have the writings of Abraham Maslow and Albert Ellis, and we have the axiological test (HVP).

Lecture V

APPLICATION OF
THE SCIENCE OF
AXIOLOGY

ABSTRACT

Having articulated his theory of formal axiology in the previous four lectures, Hartman here proceeds to describe how the theory might be applied in various real-world situations. Specifically, he discusses how formal axiology can be applied to studies of economics and political economies, including profit sharing; to international affairs, including matters of war and peace; and to personal ethics. To Hartman, nothing less than the survival of human existence depends on this.

It is my intention, in this lecture, to discuss in detail the application of the Science of Axiology to three fields which will illustrate the impact that axiological thinking has, and can have, on contemporary problems of our world. The three fields are: 1) political economy, 2) international political affairs, and 3) personal ethics. The first example, which concerns the economic system, will illustrate the relation between morality and economics. The second, which concerns the political system, especially with respect to war, will illustrate the relation between individual morality and collective immorality. The third, which concerns relations between fathers and sons, will illustrate the relation between two different moral values. It is my hope that these examples will provide a concrete view of formal axiology.

The relation between moral and economic value has been discussed in books many times over but always categorically rather than axiomatically and, consequently, has failed to lead to a new economic system. The axiom of Axiology shows that moral value has primacy over economic value. The question is how, in the face of economic reality, can this primacy be imposed? If formal axiology is correct then we should be able to observe that, in practice, economic systems function better when they are more moral and worse when they are less moral. Since the function of an economic system is the creation of wealth, then, according to our definition of "good," a good economic system is one that creates wealth and a bad economic system is one that does not create wealth. In other words, a bad economic system gives rise to poverty rather than wealth. In political economy the word "poor" is the counterpart of the word "bad" in formal axiology, and conversely, the word "rich" is the counterpart of the axiological word "good," and "wealth" the counterpart of the axiological word "goodness."

Further, since according to formal axiology, moral value has primacy over economic value, we should be able to observe in economic reality that the lack of morality in an economic system leads to impoverishment, while the existence of social morality in an economic system leads to enrichment, economically called wealth.

What is the meaning of morality in an economic system? We have defined morality as the application of intrinsic value to persons, and have shown that the human being has literally infinite value. Economic value has been defined as the application of extrinsic value to things and it was shown that things viewed extrinsically have infinitely less value than persons. Consequently, it is clear that an economic system combined with morality means the combination of the extrinsic value of things with the intrinsic value of persons.

The combination of persons and things in economic activity is called the process of production. Defined by John Locke, production is the conjunction of human labor with nature. In a factory, the raw materials enter on one side and get out the other as finished products. What has happened meanwhile? In a special manner, the raw materials have combined with human labor. The moral factor, then, in production, ought to be grafted on to human labor.

In applying the dimensions of value to human labor, it will be observed how well they fit the facts and how easily they not only order the facts but also provide an understanding of the core of economic activity.

Systematically, the acts of labor are part of an exact, calculated system in which each act is paid in accordance with its capacity and function within the system. This is labor as viewed by the Taylor system which divided work into minute acts calculated to the second and paid in fractions of cents. To this was added the army of indefatigable time-study engineers, efficiency experts, and resultant industrial managers. What does man derive from such a system? Considered as no more than a bundle of fragmented elements it is not possible for him to put his heart and soul into his work. In enterprises of this type, when a worker is asked what he is doing, his pathetic and ironical reply is usually: "Nothing, I just work here." It is natural for him not to be interested in the progress of the business, for he only works for his pay, which is by the hour, although more accurately by the second, and he will try to do the least work for the most pay. He is alienated both from himself and from the economy, and he rebels against this alienation, in deadening split-up work a la Chaplin's "Modern Times," by strikes, as in the most modern but actually antiquated new Vega factories of General Motors.

As the worker holds back his labor in this kind of work – up to 40% and more of his capacity – so the wonders of industry hold his wages; both compete in giving as little for as much as the traffic will bear. So we have two diametrically opposed forces, in the deadly struggle of the classes. This is the theory of traditional economics which culminated in Karl Marx and which treats of economic man in two opposing roles, as two opposing classes struggling only for gain; the management side has been described by Adam Smith and Ricardo, the proletarian side by Karl Marx. This is what we call the old capitalistic system. It is the application of systemic value to work. Its science is classical economics and its man is *homo oeconomicus*.

In this system there is no room for morality and therefore, according to our formal hypothesis, it should be a relatively poor system.

The application of extrinsic value to labor does not divide work into minute elements but considers work a class of functions executed by working-men. As such, each worker is a function within a class of workers ("class" in the logical and, hence, social sense), and the fulfillment of his function, using his own skill, is complemented by the functions of other workers using their skills. This system of economy and of labor is characterized by job evaluation, merit systems, and pay not for special, minute fractions of labor but for the worker's skill and ability. What is valued here are not minute acts of labor, but the worker as a member of the class of workers. Man is paid for his work without the consideration of specific jobs, as in the guaranteed annual wage, in job rotation and the like. This is part of the present capitalistic system and is a more advanced economic system than the former. Man is now considered a social, rather than merely an economic being. We call the science of this system social economy and its man *homo socialis*. In this system there are two opposing classes, labor and management, and the conflict between these classes is on the social rather than economic level: the great collective bodies of unions and industries, and a precise balance between the two.

According to our hypothesis, this system should create more wealth than the former; and it is quite clear today, since the two systems exist side by side, that the old capitalistic system based on the exploitation of labor is poorer than the newer system. The United States and other countries which have advanced in economic development are richer than the countries with economies based on the predatory capitalism of systemic value, such as South Africa, Brazil, and the pseudo-feudal countries and colonies, where fewer and fewer rich become richer and richer, and more and more poor become poorer and poorer.

More advanced, still, than the second or social stage of the economic system, is the moral stage: the application of intrinsic value to labor, out of which grows a new science, moral economics and its man, *homo moralis*.

The application of intrinsic value to labor means that the labor is considered not as a Taylorian construction, nor as a function within the class of laborers, but as a moral person of infinite value. This means that the worker gives his complete self to his work, with a sense of responsibility not only for himself but also for his colleagues, the company, and the total economy. His interest in the business will be as intense as the owner's, who also is a person of infinite moral value; and with the disappearance of the division between capital and labor, we will have a collaboration between individuals which will result in an economy that surpasses anything that we know today. To some extent, this has already occurred in North America, especially in the profit-sharing industries, which in all economic statistics are the wealthiest and best managed in every country. Moreover, they completely reverse the division of labor in a process of integration of labor: small groups of workers are responsible for whole assemblies and subassemblies, including their own quality control. The prototype of this new kind of industry is the Lincoln Electric Company in Cleveland, Ohio. Examples in Europe include the Saab automotive works in Sweden.

Labor leaders of this new moral economy, such as the late Walter Reuther and his successors, are more interested in the productivity of the economy than in the fight for wages. For progressive management, in the United States today, high wages—after the revolutionary pioneering of Henry Ford sixty years ago—participation of labor in management, job security and pensions are obvious requirements. Only the old-style businessman in the U.S. is primarily interested in profits and secondarily in supplying the market. His labor counterpart, the old-style labor leader, is primarily interested in wages and the class struggle. What the profit motive is for the old-style businessman, the struggle between the classes is for the old-style labor leader. The modern labor leaders and modern businessmen agree that they are economic and social partners with a common interest in high production and high wages, that is, in Prosperity.

This new economic procedure based on mutual interest on the part of labor and management, introduces a community of human relations between management and labor, heretofore unimagined. The human dimension becomes a new dimension in administration, as important as skill; and without the understanding of it a modern businessman will not be able to fulfill his task.

This view of human relations in business takes us into a completely new realm, far different from the old theory of industrial management and its calculations, or from viewing the economy as a whole in a mathematically finite manner. It takes us into the realm of intrinsic value whose mathematics is infinite, or, more accurately, transfinite. It can be said that the more finite mathematical calculations are applied to the field of human relations and the more narrowly correct they are, the greater the falseness of the result. The new science of human relations presupposes a transfinite analysis provided by formal axiology.

A number of examples prove this. When the establishment of a ten-minute rest period each morning and afternoon was proposed in a factory in Baltimore several years ago, the management engineers got to work with their slide rules and calculating machines in order to determine exactly what the loss of production would be as a result of these twenty minutes of rest daily, five days a week, twenty times per month, multiplied by twelve per year, for 1,200 workers, paid by the hour. On the basis of these calculations they reported that the production loss would ruin the company. However, the rest periods were established anyway, and instead of loss of production, production increased. With twenty minutes less "work" each day, more was produced than formerly. The same result was recorded in the famous Hawthorne experiments of Elton Mayo and others. The old psychotechnic methods of Taylor, which did not consider a person even as a pure economic function but as a fragment of labor subdivided into sub-fragments, without taking into account the person behind these fragments, have brought about results in which true calculations play no part. The object of the Hawthorne experiments was the study of human workers; and it was found, in general although not in particular, that no matter what methods were applied to a group under study, whether higher wages were paid or not, more hours of work required or less, whether working conditions were better or worse, the production of each group increased in every case. The reason was that the workers were being considered as human beings and they responded accordingly. The experiments also indicated that there existed a reserve of energy previously unused, good-will, and the desire to cooperate on the part of the workers. Many other examples can be given, but one more, concerning a foundry in Ohio, will suffice. This foundry operated on the following formula: 100% minus 50% equals 170%. The owner said that he stayed awake nights thinking about how he, in his "small way could do something to better the world." He finally decided to gives his workers 50% participation in the profits of his company. As a result of their greater cooperation, greater punctuality, less absenteeism, greater savings in materials, less accidents among them, production increased 40% and the profits 340%. These profits were divided in half: 170% for the workers, 170% for the owner who received 70% more than before he gave away 50% of his profits. At the same time, he lowered his price 40%.

What made all of this possible was the inclusion in the equation of the resources of human cooperation. It was an investment made in people, the employment of a previously unused economic resource, the willingness to work. This and other similar formulae are valid for some 120,000 plants in the United States and thousands in Europe, Asia, Australia, and Latin America, which have given the workers a share in the profits. All of these experiments have shown that, if human cooperation is mobilized, it is the most powerful economic resource at our disposal. Labor, viewed intrinsically, is not a commodity to be bought and sold at a price, wages, but rather the worker's investment of his own self in the company, as a true partner, and his corresponding participation in the success of the firm.

That profit-sharing, a moral system of economics, leads to greater riches than the traditional and social systems, is exemplified by the trust plan or deferred plan by which a certain percentage of the income of a company is set aside in a trust fund from which an employee receives his share on retirement. Of these, both qualitatively and quantitatively, Sears Roebuck has the most outstanding plan, with more than 200,000 members participating in its trust fund. When a Sears Roebuck employee retires after twenty-five or thirty years of service, a sort of graduation ceremony is held. I was present at a graduation in the old non-inflationary years. The employees were divided into three groups: those who had been earning up to two thousand dollars a year, those who had been earning up to three thousand, and those who had been earning up to four thousand dollars a year. On this particular occasion, some who had been earning up to two thousand dollars a year, received, after twenty-five years of service with the company, as much as thirty thousand dollars. Those who had been earning up to three thousand a year, received as much as sixty thousand dollars; and those who had been earning up to four thousand a year received up to $120,000 – and these were honest to goodness dollars. Today the results are multiplied, but the large numbers are less significant. Of course, these amounts are not paid in one lump as the U.S. government and not the retiring employee would get most of it. What makes possible such amounts as these is the increase of the fund by means of interest and investments over the course of time. The average of the individual funds of Sears Roebuck employees in the United States at that time was $40,000! In Mexico, Sears Roebuck employees had, after a number of years, more money in their individual funds than did the U.S. employees after the same length of time, because of the higher increment of the fund due to higher interest rates. When these employees retire or leave the company and take out their money, they will be, relatively speaking, rich people.

Here is a system, economically good, which creates riches for all and which already exists in many parts of the world. It is based on the infinite value of the human being and the transfinite logic of intrinsic value.

This system has nothing whatever to do with the oppositions within the old systems of capitalism and communism. It is an entirely new system, and both these old systems are developing in its direction. The methods, mentioned above, are not limited to the capitalistic system because the line dividing capital and labor no longer exists. All of these methods can be applied and are being applied within the socialist and communist systems. The change has already begun in Russia and is operating on a large scale in Yugoslavia. The difference between Russian Communism and Yugoslav Communism is precisely the difference in the degree to which the workers share in the profits and in the administration of the enterprises. There is little practical, though a legal, difference between a Yugoslav company and a cooperative in the United States in which the workers are the owners, and there are many such companies both in the United States and in other parts of the world. Neither is there much difference between the management of a Russian enterprise and an American company operating within the socio-economic system. "Man does not live by bread alone," and the Organization Man of Dudintsev's book,

may just as easily be American as Russian. Axiologically, old-style Capitalism and Communism have many
characteristics in common and, from different points of
departure, develop in the same direction. Axiologically,
we can also see how correct are the revolutionaries when
they say that poverty is unnecessary. However, the revolution that will abolish poverty is not a political but a
moral revolution. From the axiom of axiology follows
the theorem that the degree of poverty in a society is
the measure of its lack of moral and social responsibility;
the wealth of a nation is a direct function of its social
morality. It is no accident that during the Nixon Administration with its moral scandals the economy of the
United States and its currency hit rock bottom. And the
Soviet economy, throughout its 50 year history, has been
plagued by crucial shortages, most recently of wheat,
so that only massive foreign purchases avoided a fam-
ine. These two countries were victors in World War II.
Germany and Japan, on the other hand, were the losers.
But they went through a crucible of moral regeneration.
They are today the most prosperous nations after the two
giants—and without suffering their internal contradictions.

Social morality is closely connected with political
morality. That morality is the prime factor in the goodness of an economic system, that is, for the creation of
wealth, has already been demonstrated. We shall now
show the need for morality for the goodness of a political

system. Such a system is called a state. What, then, is a good state? According to the axiological axiom, a good state is a state which fulfills the definition of "state." But what is the definition of "state" and what are the properties that govern it? It was simple to define the function of an economic system, i.e. to create wealth. The definition of a state appears to be more difficult. Nevertheless, we can arrive at this definition easily if we do not recall all that has been written on this subject, but use our common sense and powers of observation, that is, the scientific method in the Galilean sense of observing the phenomena and penetrating to the essence of the subject. What is a state?

When we walk along the street or drive along the highway, it is quite clear to us what element in our surroundings belongs to the state. It is found neither in the trees nor the stores, for example, for although there are state trees and stores, they are not essential to the state. The element that belongs to the state is found in the organisms of public order, especially the police and the military. The police are in charge of keeping public order; and if I am assaulted by a thief or involved in some other kind of serious emergency, the police will help me. As a rule, we do not think of the police in terms of the function of assistance but rather in terms of the function of arrest; that is, we consider the police from the point of view of the thief and not of the peaceful citizen. From the viewpoint of the peaceful citizen, the police protects him in case of emergencies, disasters, and catastrophes, and for their services he pays through taxes. Curiously enough, the citizen pays for these services in the hope that he will never require them, that a situation never will arise that will make it necessary for him to utilize the services that he pays for throughout his life. He hopes with all his heart that others will benefit by these organisms which he pays for and that neither will he have to make use of these apparatus nor will they be concerned with him in any way. In short, he pays in order not to receive anything. The State, then, is the maintenance of an apparatus by citizens who want to have as little to do with this apparatus as possible. With the money they work so hard for, they finance the less fortunate in cases of emergency, even with the fervent desire of helping them. What is most curious is that this altruistic behavior stems from the most profound egotistical motives, somewhat like the statement I once read on a house in Bavaria: "Saint Florian, protect our town, don't burn my house, burn others down." This profound egoism leads to a most profound altruistic action in which the state exemplifies this curious situation. The principle behind this, however, is not at all curious, being one that we employ constantly in many different ways in our life. It is the principle of insurance. We pay an insurance company for exactly the same reason we pay for the police, with the fervent hope that we will never have to use it; and there is nothing we would like better than to arrive at the end of a year having lost our money. We pay the premium for the following year again in the hope that we will lose it. The principle of the state is the principle of insurance – a theory of the state rarely found in books devoted to this subject. It is a principle profoundly moral and widely used. For example, another curiosity, it is the same principle as that of lottery, except that in the case of a lottery we finance those more fortunate than we, and in the case of insurance we finance those less fortunate than we. A lottery thus is no more nor less gambling than is insurance.

In what respect is the principle of insurance, one type of which is the state, a moral principle? Simply insofar as all power channeled in the public order is focused on a person in trouble, on a person who is neither part of a system nor member of a class, but himself alone, this human being in adversity. The state and insurance are really the principle of all for one. Unfortunately, this simple situation has never been seen clearly, as has its contrary, one for all, the conformity of one to a group, or being one among many to produce collective unity. The latter is the general theory of the state today, and even the emblem of the United States contains the word *E pluribus unum*, one from many, instead of *Omnes per unum*, all for one. Today, we are living in the epoch of collectivity, and the individual does not firmly exist either in the theory or the practice of the state. Formal axiology should rescue him.

The bitterest consequence of this notion of collective unity with respect to the state is war, which leads to the greatest tension between the intrinsic value of moral man and the systemic value of the immoral state. The *raison d'état*, the Reason of the State, is amoral and usually immoral. In war, values are tuned upside down. In time of war, the most honorable man is the one who kills the greatest number of people, while in time of peace if he kills only one he gets the electric chair, is hung, or shot, or will spend a lifetime in prison. The war hero is the criminal during peacetime and vice versa. If one contends, as has been done on many occasions, that it is not people but soldiers that are killed in war, then one simply is saying that soldiers are not people, which happens to be the crux of the problem of war. Unfortunately, soldiers not only kill soldiers, but also murder people, as in My Lai.

The difference between soldiers and people is illustrated by the following little story from "Humor in Uniform" of the *Reader's Digest* (April 1973, p. 33).

> We and two other families in our neighborhood gave a party to welcome our new neighbors, a retired Army colonel and his wife. The evening was a great success, and our guests of honor expressed their appreciation over and over. 'Really, this has been just wonderful,' they exclaimed again as they were leaving. 'We do these things for each other in the Army, you know, but we didn't know that people did!'

People are educated to be good citizens and then, as soldiers, trained by their governments to use the most diabolical instruments of torture, taught by means of sacks filled with straw to slit open the maximum number of abdomens in the minimum amount of time. Our sons have been in such situations, good young men who until now had never slit open abdomens and hated the very idea – and we ourselves had taught them to hate it. What then is this sinister power that forces good people into this diabolical predicament? It is the absolute sovereignty of the nation to which we belong. Sovereignty is the expression of the principle of collectivity that makes one out of many, but there is more to it, which formal axiology explains. Sovereignty means "Superiority": it means that the nation is superior to, above and beyond, the moral law, indeed, that no law applies to it except the ones it accepts voluntarily. It is the expression of a jungle of collectivities where might is right. This is a principle completely in opposition to all existing morality – the soldier principle as against the people principle – and in opposition to all axiological definitions of good. Indeed, it corresponds to the axiological definition of evil. And its consequences are both evil—and insane.

This becomes clear when we compare the behavior of sovereign states with that of states and organizations that lack sovereignty. Each formally structured group is a whole, be it a corporation, a town, a city or a state. Obviously, it would be considered mad if the state of

Montana declared war on Idaho, or if Idaho and Montana organized the rest of the states of the Union into opposing confederations with the object of their warring against each other. It would also be considered insane if the citizens of Newark, N.J., were called up for military service to invade the territory of New York City – but this sort of thing was not considered insane during the Middle Ages when cities made war on each other with the same avidity that nations make war today. It would be equally insane if the General Motors workers in Detroit were given arms in order to conquer the Ford Motor Company. The competition between these two companies is economic and based on co-existence. On the other hand, it is not considered insane, say, for the people of France to be armed to make war against Algiers, the people of Germany to make war against Russia, the people of of Honduras against San Salvador. Nevertheless, as concerns real power, General Motors is more powerful than Algiers, Indochina, Honduras or San Salvador; its annual production is greater than any of these countries, greater than all of Scandinavia and almost half that of West Germany.

National wars appear not insane if one accepts the notion of national sovereignty – as do most people – and it does appear insane if one does not – as does an ever growing group of people. The former do not recognize, the latter do recognize, the moral evil of sovereignty, its being above and beyond the law.

What we have seen in the economic field we now see in the political field: the morally insensitive will extol sovereignty, that is, the military, while the morally sensitive will extol society, that is, the people. The former are impelled by fear, the latter by good will and faith. The division between these attitudes separates, in every nation today, neighbor from neighbor, parents from children, hard hats from teachers, town and gown, and political parties within itself. Indeed, it split the Nixon Administration straight through the middle.

If the axiological analysis is correct, then a good state, in which the insurance principle, good will, and compassion prevail, will be a better organized, economically richer, and individually more concerned society than a bad state, which is victim to sovereignty, the military, and which cuts down social welfare. Again, we have the dramatic examples of Germany and Japan on the one hand, and Russia and the United States on the other. The former two were by the Victors constitutionally forbidden to have a military establishment, that is, their sovereignty was limited. They could channel all their resources into the civil society, and as a result soared ahead in political savvy and economic growth. The Victors on the other hand, both in the United States and the Soviet Union, suffer from extreme military expenditures, a lethal nuclear race, economic shortages and dislocations, racial strife, a drying up of the civil society – e.g., the United States is in 13th rank among the peoples of the earth in infant mortality – and contradictions which can only lead to chaos.

What is the difference between the insanity of arming General Motors against the Ford Motor Company and the rationality of arming Germany against Russia or Honduras against San Salvador? The reasons are that these last are sovereign nations, and sovereignty is something more than mere unity. The nation considered as sovereign is not just seen as a unit but is endowed with that strange kind of power which disregard of the law gives the criminal. The sovereignty of the democratic collectives is a fiction masterfully constructed by Rousseau, as the general will, *la volonté géneralé*, whose properties are neither more nor less than the same properties that belonged to the absolute monarch. In the great democratic revolutions in France, the United States, Russia and other countries, the absolute sovereignty of the autocratic Sovereign was crushed as far as domestic matters were concerned, but remained intact as far as foreign relations were concerned. The new democracies which succeeded the absolute monarch claimed national sovereignty, as had their erstwhile King or Emperor. But since there was no longer a sovereign as a single physical person, sovereignty had to be constructed, and any connection with concrete reality had to be ignored. Therefore, it remained as a fiction, as a construction, and axiologically it is a systemic value.

As a result, all nations today, democratic or totalitarian, have, as refers to their foreign relations, that is, their relations with each other, all the characteristics of the autocratic prince of ancient times. According to the theories of Hobbes and the practice of those times, the prince had totalitarian rights over his subjects. He was above the law, the sole moral judge, and it was sinful for the subject to make judgements based on his own conscience. Further, the sovereign prince had absolute power over all property, and his subjects owed him total obedience. Rousseau transferred all of these characteristics to the prince-less collective, the collective that arose out of the revolution. This being the case, as regards external relations, all the revolutions of the past from the American, French, the African and South American, up to the Russian, were futile, and the international situation is exactly the same as if these revolutions had never taken place.

The natural expression of this state of things is war. In time of war, the force that is imposed by a republican quasi-democratic sovereignty, is the same as that of autocratic and monarchic sovereignty: the citizen owes complete obedience to the collective of the nation as his sovereign, in exactly the same way his forebearers owed obedience to the absolute monarch. What was criminal in terms of his personal and moral life, was heroic in terms of this obedience and is still, even though the sovereign is no longer a single monarch but a national collective.

Nevertheless, from the point of view of axiology the transference of sovereignty from the person of the prince to the popular will is of utmost significance, for, as has been said, the popular will is a fiction, a construction, and therefore is subject only to systemic valuation. Axiologically, sovereignty has infinitely less value, in the exact meaning of our definition of infinite, than the moral value of the individual person. This leads to the inevitable conclusion that the individual person must reject the exigencies of a fiction which works against him and which is contrary to what he is, a moral being, the being who contains the infinity of intrinsic value. Axiologically, it is infinitely evil to kill another human being or to use violence against him for the sake of an idea, a system or any other abstraction. This represents the systemic devaluation of intrinsic value as symbolized by the formula I_S, which was mentioned earlier. The alternative is, of course, a moral view of sovereignty in which *la volonté géneralé* is focused on the moral person, as in the principle of insurance.

Another extremely important aspect is that to kill a human being for the sake of an idea means that the end justifies the means. This proposition, axiologically, is infinitely bad because the means are concrete and the end is a thought. The concrete, as we have seen, as intrinsic value or even as extrinsic value, is infinitely more valuable than a thought, which has systemic value. What counts exclusively is the means and not the end. This is the doctrine of Gandhi which led to his method of *Satyagraha* or non-violence. It is also the doctrine of

Jesus Christ, that we should conquer evil by good not by another evil.

Formal axiology helps us understand these often mis-understood words, which mean that against one value must be pitted a better value, and that only a better value can suppress a worse value. It means that systemic value must be overcome by extrinsic and intrinsic values. This further means that we should be creative in all situations and perceive the germ of good even in the worst situation. It is precisely what Abraham Lincoln meant when, asked why he was so kind to his enemies, he replied: "Am I not annihilating my enemies be making friends of them?" It is the doctrine of Castellio who, when Calvin burned Servetus in the name of faith, wrote: "To kill a man in the name of faith is not the defense of faith but the murder of a man." In the same way, axiology obliges us to say today: "To burn men, women and children in the name of a cause, is not the defense of the cause but the murder of men, women and children."

Scientific axiology, based on purely formal equations, thus arrives at truly revolutionary results. It ought to be destined, and I believe it is, to bring forth a new moral world. For the real revolutions are not those fought in the streets, but those of the spirit.

Two accounts, one imaginary and one real, will serve to show, respectively, the consequences that could result, on the one hand, from our failure and, on the other, from a method towards moral success in this world. The first account can be found in Nevil Shute's novel *On the Beach*, in which the beach represents the ocean of time on whose shores the last waves are lapping and dying in the sand. The beach is that of Melbourne, Australia, the southernmost city of the world, where the people are living out the last weeks and months of their lives. Life on earth is about to disappear due to a short but devastating atomic war in the northern hemisphere, and the polluted atmosphere is slowly moving southward with the winds and currents. In latitude after latitude, in city after city, human and animal life is dying as a result of sickness produced by radiation, a kind of cholera which begins with nausea, vomiting, diarrhea, increasingly violent spasms and, finally, death from exhaustion. Australia, like the other southern nations, distributes cyanide pills to those who want them, to help them through their last agonizing hours, so that they may die peacefully in their beds, the whole earth going to sleep, mankind ending, "not with a bang, but a whimper," as T. S. Eliot says in the motto of the book.

Some ask themselves, as we certainly would, why life on earth must come to such a ridiculous end. The only answer is, "We have been too silly to deserve a world like this." After poisoning their child and about to swallow their own pills, Lieutenant Holmes and his wife, Mary, ask each other if anyone might have prevented the course of events, and the Lieutenant says: "I don't know, some kinds of silliness you just can't stop. If a couple of hundred

million people all decide that their national honor re-
quires them to drop cobalt bombs upon their neighbor,
well, there's not much that you or I can do about it. The
only possible hope would have been to educate them out
of their silliness."

Thus, life on Earth ends in a paradox: a race that has
reached the acme of intellectual development destroys
itself willingly in abysmal stupidity. This paradox must
puzzle to the point of mystery any future visitor to this
planet, as it does, forty-five thousand years after the catastrophe, the Select Exploratory Mission, whose six-
volume report, *The Rise and Annihilation of Earth-Life*,
fell, by some spatiotemporal wizardry, into the hands
of the managing editor of the *Washington Post and Times
Herald*, Alfred Friendly, who reviewed it on June 26,
1955, where you can read it. Forty-five thousand years
after the catastrophe, "Earth is once again verdant with
forest and grass, with even the once devastated areas hid-
den under dense foliage. In one sense it is a singularly
beautiful planet. But in another, more impressive sense it
is the ultimate in horror. Over the face of this planetary
paradise there is no free-moving life. There is no eye,
no ear, no hand, no football, no intelligent thing." Even
greater than the horror is the mystery. The more the
Mission "discovered about life on Earth the less it was
able to explain its extinction."

> Each discovery reported, each deduction sub-
> stantiated, each piece of the puzzle rightly

fitted into place only serves to deepen the mystery: Here was a civilization of great advancement, motivated as all life must be by the burning desire to survive, accomplished in engineering and vastly knowledgeable in science, and esteeming the loftiest philosophical standards—which nevertheless knowingly destroyed itself. "Knowingly" is used advisedly. It is at the root of the enigma. A team headed by the Mission deputy himself makes a brilliant and irrefutable proof (Vol. II, pp. 560-719) that Earth-man could not have escaped knowing that the neutron emission from two hundred and forty-odd macro-fission-fusion reactions would fatally empoison virtually all life then extant on Earth. The proof comes from the fact that the knowledge and techniques necessary to create a giant fission and/or fusion reaction necessary include the knowledge of the degree of radio-activity that results, and its effects on life forms.

So for the Report: that the technically so highly developed Earth-man was morally silly to the point of playing with cosmic devices as a child plays with toys, the Select Exploratory Mission could not imagine. Yet this was the situation.

It is, let us be clear about it, our situation at this very moment. The reason is, again very simply, that there are two entirely different kinds of knowledge, material knowledge and moral knowledge, and that up to this day we have developed the former and neglected the latter. The solution, then, for us humans on Earth, with our destiny still in our hands, our future still wide open, Earth still beckoning to us to continue the grand adventure of life we share with our brothers and sisters in the Universe—the solution is simply to close the time lag between material and moral knowledge and to develop the latter as we have the former. It means the creation of a moral science.

The new science is well on the way and is being taught already. We have found that learning these laws changes the character of the young people, makes them more aware, more awake, and more sensitive. As a matter of fact, we have found that it changes whole families, bringing them happiness and insight. Let me mention only one such case. One of my students told me a week or so before the term papers were due that the writing of that paper was "the most important thing in my life." When I got the paper the title was "Homecoming of a Son." The subject was, in short, that through learning the various value dimensions he had found that he had never loved his parents. He had been ashamed of them for being workers. Learning the true values – that intrinsic value has nothing to do with what a person does, but only with who he is—he had seen the injustice he had done them. He wanted to correct it, but the problem was how to do it without showing them that he had never loved them before. The paper was about the method he evolved to overcome this difficulty, how he showed them his love, and how this changed the whole atmosphere in the home from one of indifference and tension to one of love. "Harmony and continual laughter prevailed." He did all this during the Christmas vacation, and he wrote the paper while he acted out its content. To read it was a thrilling experience, like a miracle consciously wrought. About two weeks later he came to me with a letter from his mother. She wrote that such strange and wonderful things had happened during the vacation that she and his dad had been thinking and talking about what it was, and they had come to the conclusion – that they had never really loved him. "I have felt for years that somewhere along the line Daddy and I failed you in some way....Life is sure funny, isn't it? You go through the years while life is passing you by thinking you are doing what's right and yet you are blind to what really is happening around you."

This seems to me a perfect description of our present situation. We are blind to the true values all around and within us. If the whole world would learn the true values the way that young man and his family learned them, our troubles would largely be over, the equilibrium in human affairs would be restored, and the scene on the beach at Melbourne would never take place.

These, then, are the two pictures of the world of the future: a world of life and love, and a world of death and desolation. One or the other of these worlds will and must be ours. Either what I have said is fiction and what Nevil Shute has said is prediction, or what Nevil Shute has said is – and will remain – fiction and what I have said is prediction. The sputniks and satellites, whirling high above us at this moment, spell either our doom or our destiny.

This, then, is our extraordinary opportunity. We may go on spending our money to develop hydrogen and co-balt bombs, make the scene at Melbourne come true, and give the men from Outer Space their opportunity to write the six-volume report, or we may use a fraction of this money – hardly more than the cost of some tiny gadget in an intercontinental missile – to concentrate the energies of a dozen or so people on human survival. The choice is ours, and it may be final.

Lightning Source UK Ltd.
Milton Keynes UK
UKHW010718030622
403942UK00001B/160